Breaking the Ice

Breaking the Ice

An Arctic Odyssey

Arnold Ruskell

Foreword by James Houston

Shoreline

Breaking the Ice: An Arctic Odyssey

© Arnold Ruskell, 1997

All photographs from the author's collection. Cover photo of mother and child reprinted with permission of *The Beaver*.

Printed and bound in Canada by Marc Veilleux Imprimeur, Inc.

Published by Shoreline, 23 Ste-Anne, Ste-Anne-de-Bellevue, Quebec, Canada H9X 1L1. Phone/fax: 514-457-5733
E-mail: bookline@total.net

Dépôt légal: Bibliothèque nationale du Québec and National Library of Canada

Acknowledgements:

I am indebted to my wife, Sheila, for many hours of patient editing, proof-reading and encouragement, and to the Reverend Phil Gandon, who steered me through the intricacies of the word processor and rescued me on many occasions. Without their able assistance, my book might never have been completed.

Canadian Cataloguing in Publication Data

Ruskell, Arnold, 1919-
    Breaking the ice: an Arctic odyssey

ISBN 0-9698752-9-0

1. Ruskell, Arnold, 1919- 2. Inuit--Canada.
3. Canada, Northern--History. 4. Missionaries--Canada, Northern--Biography. I. Title.

BV2813.R88A3 1997   971.9'03   C95-920832-1

To the memory of

Morris and Bernice Wright

in happy recollection of Chimo days together

Contents

Foreword ~ 9
Preface ~ 11
My Early Years ~ 14
First Impressions ~ 23
Getting Adjusted ~ 34
Christmas Day, 1946 ~ 41
Trading at the Post ~ 43
Travelling in the Bush Country ~ 46
The Dog Team ~ 59
Photographs ~ 65
Building an Igloo ~ 81
Christmas Day in an Igloo on the Open Tundra ~ 84
Map of Eastern Arctic ~ 89
Fifteen Hundred Miles by Dog Team: A Winter's Journey ~ 90
Fort Chimo to Lake Harbour ~ 113
New Beginnings ~ 120
Christmas Day on Baffin Island ~ 125
Winter Quarters on the Barren Lands ~ 131
A Day in the Life of the Inuit ~ 135
Adrift on an Ice Pan ~ 141
From Feast to Famine ~ 146
Farewell and Retrospection ~ 154

Foreword

During our times in the Arctic, Arnold Ruskell had a quick, ready smile and wore a well-trimmed beard in the grand style of the King of Sweden. He was the most likeable missionary whom I ever knew in the Ungava (now called Arctic Quebec) and later at Kingmerok on Baffin Island. Arnold always had a good deal of fun and merriment to him, perhaps because he had served as a curate in a parish in the south of Ireland before his Arctic ventures began.

He was a vigorous, dedicated traveller, often ranging over two thousand kilometres by dog team during the winter and spring months, and perhaps half that distance aboard Inuit boats in the ice-clogged seas during each brief Arctic summer. Seeing him covering such territory came as no surprise to those who came to know Arnold, for he had been a noted quarter-mile runner at Trinity College, Dublin, and kept in lean, hard shape.

When Arnold undertook one particular great journey, he was the second non-native ever to attempt it. He travelled from Payne Bay, on the western shore of Ungava Bay, across the vast, uninhabited inland plain to Povungnituk, on the east coast of Hudson Bay, then south to Inukjuak. The dog team driver, who travelled with him on that perilous trek, later marvelled that Arnold had not ridden across. The Inuk driver explained that the *avaoktayivi* (missionary) had run almost all the way, usually well out in front of the dogs. Inuit admired Arnold for that vivacity and other reasons. They said they had never known any Inuit or *kallunait* with that kind of drive and fleet-footed energy.

On Baffin Island, he and I travelled east to west and west to east but never together. We did, however, gladly accept each other's hospitality at the other end of our long sled journeys to Inuit camps. We became friends.

We two have grown old now, still revelling by mail or telephone about those far-off times when we lived in the Eastern Arctic. In spite of a few hardships, our northern days are fondly remembered as perhaps the best and most vigorous periods of our lives.

James Houston
Former Administrator, West Baffin Island, NWT, Canada

Preface

In 1946, as a young man of twenty-seven, I entered the Canadian north to serve the Anglican Church in a missionary capacity. The following chapters are the story of my life, adventures and observations, during the five-year period when I worked among the Inuit. My narrative deals with the eastern Arctic only, as my experience rests entirely with the people of that area.

The book is neither a religious work nor a scholarly treatise; rather it is an evocation of that part of the world as I saw it fifty years ago. It is a factual account taken from my diaries written at Kuujjuaq (Fort Chimo) and Lake Harbour. Perhaps it will serve as a link between past and present. Undeniably, it records a way of life which no longer exists.

The Inuit are a people - they share land, speech and customs. When I was in the north, they were called Eskimos. However, in Canada today we refer to them as the "Inuit," a word meaning "people." It is the plural of the proper noun "Inuk" which denotes "man," more correctly, "*the* man," a person supreme and without equal in his own land. No one who has lived in the Arctic for any period of time would ever contemplate challenging the Inuit skill and expertise in dealing with the demands of everyday life under the most basic conditions.

It is probable that the Inuit are of Asiatic origin. Certainly they bear a strong physical resemblance to many Orientals - small stature, similar colouring, high cheekbones, small hands and feet. Anthropologists believe that many centuries ago the Inuit may have migrated from Asia across the Bering Strait, perhaps when it was a solid land mass. Some settled in Alaska, others continued into the Canadian Arctic. Today they are to be found in both places as well as Labrador, Arctic Quebec and Greenland.

Solely from a diocesan point of view, the Canadian Inuit are divided into two broad categories: eastern and western. Roughly, the demarcation line runs from a central point in northern Saskatchewan to

Baker Lake, Gjoa Haven, McClintock Channel and Melville Sound. This diocesan division can again be subdivided into the bush country Inuit and those who live beyond the tree line in the barren lands. However, Canadian Inuit language and culture cannot be separated quite so neatly. Ethnologists now speak of three geographic and cultural areas: western (around the Mackenzie Delta), central (Coppermine to Igloolik) and eastern (where I worked.)

The Inuit syllabary, Inuktitut, has been adapted from the language of the Cree Indians. In common with many other languages, the Inuit tongue is divided into numerous dialects. There is a particularly marked difference between east and west, although short association usually makes comprehension possible. I was to encounter a considerable variation in Inuktitut when the bishop, who had spent most of his ministry in the western Arctic, came on his annual visitation. My people, who lived in the east, found him hard to understand, although natural reticence prevented them from making any such comment during his visit. In addition to the east-west division, I discovered slight changes in dialect when I moved from Fort Chimo to Lake Harbour. Some words used in one settlement were unknown in the other at that time. Such distinctions in the areas which I covered were not a problem - even for me with my somewhat limited grasp of the language.

Within recent years, many settlements in the Canadian Arctic have been given Inuit names - recognizing the importance of the Inuit as a people. In the 1940s, which is the time frame of this book, few Inuit spoke English, so the white man's appellation for their settlements was to them meaningless.

By 1946 the Inuit, on the whole, were Christian, so my task was not to convert but to sustain. During the past century, many Christian clergy of varying faiths had devoted their lives to missionary work in the Arctic. Most notable among the Anglican priests was the Reverend E.J. Peck, "The Apostle to the Eskimos," who founded the mission at Little Whale River in 1876. While there, he transcribed parts of the New Testament and *The Book of Common Prayer* to syllabics. He was a gifted linguist who left a volume of Inuit grammar as a further legacy.

During my time in the north, I was aware that some of the people under my care still clung to aspects of their old religion - a fact I did not find troubling or disturbing. The Christian religion has its basis in Judaism. Certain elements of that faith are still found in Christianity today and we are enriched by them. Just as the Indians had their medicine men, so the Inuit had their shamans - people who combined the office of priest, prophet and medical practitioner. They were the intermediaries between the Inuit and the spirit world. In the old Inuit religion there were many spirits whose supernatural powers endowed simple objects (such as sticks and stones) as well as animals and the elements. It was always necessary to appease the deities lest they become hostile and destroy the balance of the environment. It was not surprising to find these influences in their religious observances and daily activities. One practical outcome of such ideas was the Inuit refusal to shoot more game than was actually needed at the time. Great care had to be taken not to anger the spirits of dead animals, as it was feared that these spirits might retaliate, causing illness and food shortages. During my time in the north I always applauded the careful use of natural resources.

The Inuit shared to some extent the Christian concept of a future life. Their idea of "a large house on high which is full of light" corresponded to heaven. Such a basic belief, common to both people, made at least one aspect of Christian doctrine more acceptable. Death to them was the passageway to another conscious existence, a better place with neither ice nor snow. That concept may have enabled them to face daily perils with a stoic's calm and courage.

This, then, in brief, was the land and the people I had chosen for the next five years. It was to be an unforgettable experience, laced with vivid memories which have endured for nearly half a century.

My Early Years

The lure of the Arctic! It has a fascination which defies description. Stand in the wide-open spaces of the high Arctic and see the aurora borealis (northern lights) with its blue-green shafts of light dancing across the sky. Witness the awesome silence of the rolling tundra and look into eternity. See a roving wolf cross the barren lands in search of food and hear its plaintive note pierce the thin air. Travel by dog team in the depth of winter when the sun scarcely combs the horizon and the eerie light of the moon casts weird shadows on the surface of the snow. Drive in the teeth of blinding snow for several days, with visibility virtually zero, and keep on track. Lose touch with the sled when it strikes a small island of hard-packed snow on a glassy lake and overturns, dragging the dogs in its wake perilously close to open water. Catapult into a lake when the rear of the sled crashes through the ice and one's clothes, in a matter of seconds, resemble a coat of armour, then continue the trip lashed on the sled like a piece of excess baggage - all in fifty degrees below zero. Find oneself afloat on an ice pan drifting out to sea with no visible means of getting back again. Travel down the bed of a gentle mountain stream in winter, with the dogs in full cry, bring the team to an abrupt standstill by ramming the side of the sled against a boulder, thus avoiding a flight over a 75-foot frozen waterfall. Cross floating ice cakes in a desperate effort to reach home before breakup.

Such have been my experiences and more, so how does one attempt to tell the story of five years among the people in the far reaches of Canada's north? Perhaps it begins best with some reference to my Irish childhood and formative years, in a land of lilting voices and gentle climate.

I was born and brought up in "The Garden of Ireland" as County Wicklow is known. The scenic beauty of Glendalough and the Seven Churches, the Vale of Avoca and the Meeting of the Waters compares more than favourably with the best that Ireland has to offer.

Family Home, County Wicklow, Ireland

My father was Irish, my mother a Scot. They met during her visit to a married sister living in County Wicklow. Evidently my father was instantly smitten, as he remarked to someone, "That's the girl I'm going to marry!" He was almost twice her age - a fact not unusual at the time. Traditionally, Irishmen did not marry young; probably economics influenced the national trend.

We were a family of six children and led a very pleasant, country-style life. Pleasures were simple, but I never remember being bored. We went to church by pony and trap on Sunday mornings with our parents. Regardless of the weather, we walked to Sunday School in the afternoons - a round trip of four miles. We all had bicycles, but it was not considered proper to use them on Sundays. My mother's Scottish Presbyterian background certainly influenced our upbringing.

School holidays were real holidays for us all. Occasionally, just for fun, we would help drawing in the hay, but there was never any thought of taking a summer job at the expense of someone who desperately needed the work and the money.

Half a century later, it may sound a very rarefied existence. It was never that at all; it simply was the way of life in those days. Labour was cheap and the work force abundant. Higher education was not so available as it is today and domestic service provided an opportunity for girls who had no other skills or prospects. Parents of large families were delighted to see girls suitably placed in comfortable houses with good food and clothing provided - items which were seldom available at home.

It is not my purpose to speak about the political situation in Ireland today. Suffice it to say that the Ireland of the present time is very different from the land of my childhood between the two world wars. In those early years, Protestant and Roman Catholic lived in apparent harmony. There was little evidence, certainly on the surface, of hatred and bitterness. In fact, my father never employed a Protestant; from the men who worked on the farm to the maids in the house, all, without exception, were Roman Catholic. They were much more reliable and were unswervingly loyal to the family.

After we had driven two governesses to distraction, my father said "Enough of this," or words to that effect, and promptly packed my older brother and me off to boarding school. I was ten years old at the time.

We were sent first of all to a small preparatory school in suburban Dublin, and later to St. Andrew's College. After a few years there, my brother and St. Andrew's had had enough of each other. He left school and I went on to Portora in Northern Ireland where my eldest brother had been educated. In those days the border between north and south presented no problems.

I look back on that time as the happiest of my school days. I still keep in touch with some of the friends I made there. Portora was a Royal Foundation, established in 1618, and when I was there many of the buildings and furnishings looked as if they might have been original. There were well-known names among the old boys: Henry Francis Lyte, the hymn writer, and at the other end of the spectrum, Oscar Wilde.

The Great Hall was virtually the centre of school life. Ranging around its walls were a series of boards recording the names of boys who had won scholarships to Trinity College, Dublin. One of the headmasters, an Anglican clergyman of narrow outlook, insisted that Wilde's literary achievements had been totally compromised by his turbulent domestic life. Standards of those days were strict indeed and immoral behaviour, with the ensuing publicity and a gaol sentence, was scarcely a good example for teenage boys. Accordingly, the entire board was erased and then repainted, leaving a space where Oscar's name should have appeared. For some unaccountable reason, the spacing was misjudged so that when the next headmaster took over, a man of liberal views who had the offending words reinstated, the name Oscar Wilde stood out more prominently than ever. Genius, even slightly tarnished, must have its place in history.

At the age of twelve, while still in preparatory school, I decided to enter the ministry. I cannot claim that my call was quite so dramatic as that of St. Paul. Rather, it took the form of "a still, small voice," but it was unmistakable. My mind was made up and I never wavered; I was quite convinced that a life of service to others was to be my role. Indeed, my formative years were a training ground for what lay ahead.

As I was destined for holy orders, extra Greek was now added to my curriculum. Portora, particularly, had a good reputation for the classics, and a number of the students who studied Greek had no intention of entering theology. Oscar Wilde is a case in point.

The boarders - it was almost exclusively a boarding school - were required to do an hour's prep in Steele Hall, nine-fifteen to ten-fifteen on Sunday mornings, half an hour reading the Bible and half an hour writing letters home. Another senior student, also a prospective ordinand, and I were excused on the grounds that we would spend the hour with the senior classics master studying the Greek New Testament. Looking back on those days, I can now well appreciate his kindness in allowing us to invade his sanctum sanctorum. The only escape for staff who lived in the school was the peace and quiet of their private quarters.

We were dismissed promptly at ten-fifteen in time to put on our Sunday best and join the entire school now assembled on the front terrace. The school uniform consisted of a black jacket (blazer), grey shirt, school tie and grey trousers; but Sunday attire was more formal: black jacket, striped trousers (the director's suit of today), white shirt, school tie, grey coat and gloves, topped off with a tall silk hat. In summer term we wore hard straw hats - "boaters" as we called them. At ten-thirty we were called to order: juniores priores, house prefects and school prefects. The head prefect had the dubious distinction of taking up the rear with a senior staff member.

We walked down the winding pathway, crocodile fashion, bound for divine service at the Cathedral at eleven.

The school is strategically situated on a hill and has a commanding view of lower Lough Erne and the market town of Enniskillen. The opening stanza of the school song, which I can still recite from memory, expresses it thus:

> Alone she stands upon her hill
> Living her cloistered, peaceful life;
> Remote, serene, a place apart,
> Above the shouting and the strife.

I considered myself an average, all-round student, and my intentions for holy orders did not mean that I spent my days in an ivory tower poring over the scriptures. I was always very keen on sports and took a particular interest in athletics, rugby, shooting, fishing and boxing - in that order. I dabbled in tennis and swimming. The Officers' Training Corps was a prominent part of school life and most of us joined up. The discipline appealed to me. There were weekly parades and each cadet was responsible for his own uniform. During the summer term we went on manoeuvres and at the conclusion of each school year a contingent joined British schools at an OTC campsite in England. One year I went with them to York. We had a bet among us: who would "pinch" - not to be confused with stealing - the greatest number of swagger sticks. (Collecting these canes was the "in" thing.) With a haul of fifteen, I must have come close to topping the list. Every school sported a swagger stick. The school crest was engraved on the silver knop. Some were very handsome.

At school, there was considerable emphasis on discipline and many of us, myself included, have vivid recollections of corporal punishment. The rod was not spared for those who stepped out of line. Caning wasn't a case of holding out one's hand - nothing quite so civilized! We were ordered to bend over and touch our toes and were given "three of the best" on you-know-where! One was sorely tempted, on hearing the swish of the cane as muscles were being flexed, to turn round. A fourth crack was the penalty.

I am all in favour of this system and can speak from experience. I happened to mention to my father one holidays that I had been caned the previous term. His only comment: "You probably deserved it." I bear no deep, psychological scars as a result. It is my belief that if more discipline were administered in our schools today, it might reap valuable dividends in the future. Among the students in the mid-1930s, bullies and smart-alecs were summarily dealt with; even the head prefect had the authority to use the cane on such occasions.

It was fortunate when I entered the University of Dublin, Trinity College, that my future profession had already been decided. It was my intention to take a degree in classics. Latin was compulsory in the schools which I attended. By the time I reached College, I had about six years of classical Greek as a credit and several years of New Testament Greek. My tutor wouldn't hear of it; he believed that a university education was designed to broaden one's outlook, so he recommended philosophy. It was not just a suggestion. I was hardly in a position to argue the point.

Training for the future continued apace during my college days. Early on, I was commissioned as a lay reader by the Archbishop of Dublin, and the rector of my home parish took a personal interest in me. It was he who instructed me how to read and take services. I was joined by his son, now my brother-in-law, who was also studying for the priesthood. It was this same rector who probably sowed the seed of service in the mission field. (He had spent a number of years in the Canadian Church.)

Trinity provided another happy period of my life. Obviously, some study was necessary, but there were also many opportunities for athletic pursuits. At boarding school I had specialized in track and field. As an undergraduate, my secret ambition was to captain the Athletic Club and win an Irish quarter-mile title - 400 metres. Heady stuff for an eighteen-year-old, but we all have our wild fantasies!

My delusions of grandeur encouraged me to train very hard, and there is no doubt that the physical stamina I gained on the athletic field served me well in later life - particularly in the frozen wastes of Canada's north. I graduated in arts and theology and was ordained to the sacred ministry in 1942 and subsequently licensed for the assistant curacy of Clonmel, County Tipperary.

Life was so different in those days. One was not given any choice about future employment. I was simply summoned by the Regius Professor of Divinity and told, "Ruskell, you will be going to Clonmel." I said, "Thank you, sir," and went.

Those were golden years. I was a paying guest at a lovely old Georgian house in the country and parted with the ridiculous sum of £5 per week for board and lodging, and for an additional £2 was able to keep a horse for fox hunting. As I had to spend most mornings improving my mind and preparing in the first year for the priest's orders examination, I often rose early to exercise the animal and sometimes enjoyed a day's hunting with the Tipperary foxhounds. The rector viewed my weekend activities with alarm. A broken bone on Saturday could have put me out of action for the next day's services. Country parishes were not easy to fill at short notice.

I had always done a bit of riding at home, but was not nearly so keen about fox hunting as my older brothers. They both rode very well, following the example of my father who was an excellent horseman. I simply wasn't in their league. However, in Clonmel I soon made friends with a hunting family and they encouraged me to join them. Before long I, too, was an addict.

The hunting season concluded with the annual Hunt Ball. And what a finale! It was a gala occasion. The ball was usually held at the house of the Master of Hounds; invitations were issued not only to members, but also to the followers of adjoining packs. It was a very formal occasion and people dressed accordingly. The traditional black and white for the men was enlivened by a number of scarlet tailcoats, lapels emblazoned with the distinctive colour of each hunt. A band hired especially for the occasion inspired people to dance energetically most of the evening. Parched throats enjoyed frequent trips to the bar and the buffet supper was always a lavish affair.

Tipperary was a sportsman's paradise. Pheasant, grouse and partridge abounded and landowners sometimes were kind enough to include me in a shooting party. Wing shooting appealed particularly; it required more skill and accuracy and always seemed a bit more sporting than going out for larger game.

There were frequent tennis parties organized by different groups, and occasionally we played at a house called "Knocklofty" owned by the Donoughmores. Years later, Lord Donoughmore was kidnapped and held for ransom by the IRA. Today the house is a hotel. The family has moved to England.

Clonmel was an interesting old market town in the centre of an agricultural area and a number of land-owning families dotted the countryside. Inevitably, a few characters stand out, among them the Duke of St. Albans who attended a neighbouring parish. A direct descendant of Nell Gwyn and Charles II, he was immensely proud of his ancestry, and his behaviour at times could be quite amusing, even a bit eccentric. I was exposed to some of it when my rector and I were called upon to fill in at his church during an interregnum. Before service began, he could sometimes be seen going up and down the aisle asking the parishioners to make change so that he would have a suitable sum to put on the collection plate. If no one could oblige, he did not hesitate to help himself when the plate was passed should his contribution seem overly generous. The St. Albans family always sat at the end of their pew close to the wall so that the Duke could prop himself up in comfort during the sermon. Settling in for what might be a long siege by his standards, he would close his eyes, opening one hopefully from time to time to see if the preacher had finally made his point. If not, he would drop off again. A long-winded discourse inevitably prompted the production of his pocket watch. It was one thing to see him pull it out, but when he began to shake it vigorously, even the most gifted orator (and I was not one) felt somewhat intimidated and the sermon usually came to an abrupt end.

Looking back, it all seems a fairy-tale existence - one which produced a great deal of pleasure but involved very little effort. Actually my duties were clearly defined; the work had to be done, and excuses were not acceptable. A curacy was a type of internship - a training which helped to establish one's pattern for the future. The mornings were devoted to reading and preparation for sermons, and visiting occupied most afternoons. Rectors could be quite demanding, sometimes one felt unnecessarily so, but my free time was my own and I certainly took advantage of every moment. I do remember vividly, bicycling 30 miles on a Sunday evening after service to catch the train. Occasionally, I tried to spend my day off (Monday) with my family, but I was never allowed to miss Evensong, which certainly would have simplified travel arrangements. Social life and sporting activities gave me an introduction to people whom I might not otherwise meet. I saw them, as indeed they saw me, in a totally different context. We stood on equal ground as it were, abandoning the stereotyped roles of priest and parishioner. I came to know them as individuals, not just as faces in the congregation or as people I passed on the street. I could have remained in that parish quite happily for the rest of my life, but thought it advisable to move to Dublin to gain more experience in my chosen profession. I was really too comfortable.

It may seem ridiculous today in an era when few clergy serve curacies at all, but at that time in Ireland a second curacy was quite usual. Monkstown parish church, on the outskirts of Dublin, provided me with a different type of experience. It was a large, lively parish with many children and an active youth programme. One of my many duties included the Confirmation classes at the Hall School for girls. The teenagers and I, always under the watchful eye of the headmistress, gathered in her drawing room for an hour each week. I have never been quite able to decide whether the chaperon was there to protect the girls from me or me from the girls!

During my time in the parish, the rector died. According to church procedure, I automatically resigned when the new incumbent arrived. For some time I had wanted to serve in the mission field, and now was my opportunity. I made application to an English missionary society which had a representative in Dublin. There was a choice at that time between the Canadian Arctic and Madras, India. I chose the former as I had always preferred cold to heat. Perhaps a slender reason for redirecting one's life, but it was a decision I never regretted.

The year was 1945. There was a big problem - the war was over and with the repatriation of troops, and war brides going to join husbands, a passage to Canada was out of the question. It seemed that there might well be a year to fill in and so, remembering my carefree days at Trinity, I went up to Keble College, Oxford, for a course in systematic theology. At that time the college attracted graduates and undergraduates with a particular interest in the Church and theology generally. Its architecture was unprepossessing, but the interior of the chapel boasted the famous Holman Hunt painting, "The Light of the World."

I made a friend at Worcester College who supplied me with a horse and we went fox hunting on a few occasions with a local pack. I managed to do a bit of running as well. Unfortunately, a badly sprained Achilles tendon, just before a major event, made any serious competition impossible.

First Impressions

My D-day finally arrived. I set sail for Halifax, Nova Scotia, in July 1946, aboard the SS *Aquitania*, which in the early years of the war had been converted into a troop ship. I was fortunate to get a berth. The ship was extremely crowded with returning troops, and the crossing incredibly rough. Among the passengers were several MPs and Sir Anthony Eden. He gave the address at the morning service on the Sunday and spoke highly of Canada's contribution to the war effort.

Midafternoon on the fifth day, we were within sight of Halifax and soon could see the tremendous crowd of people anxiously waiting to welcome home the troops. Several speedboats came out to meet us, circled the ship a few times and returned to port. Presently we drew near. The ship's massive frame slowly glided in towards the dock. The ovation of the crowd was deafening. Aircraft roared overhead, bands were playing, flags flying, handkerchiefs waving and large streamers with the words "Welcome Home" imprinted on them fluttered in the breeze. It was all most impressive.

Understandably, no private passengers were permitted to leave until the military had disembarked. The steady stream of officers, men and women seemed endless. Finally, three hours after docking, we were allowed to go ashore. Two years later, the 45,000-ton liner made her last voyage - to the Clyde to be dismantled after many years' service.

I set off for the Canadian National Railway Bureau to collect my ticket for Toronto. It was twelve midnight when I boarded the Pullman for Montreal, then Canada's largest city. I decided to spend a few days seeing the sights, realizing that the opportunity might not come my way again.

I telephoned the Arctic Diocesan office in Toronto to say that I would not arrive until later in the week. The secretary, who answered the phone, was horrified. I could almost read her mind: How could anyone, particularly a fledgling missionary, dare to stand up the bishop!

In sepulchral tones she said, "Oh, Mr. Ruskell," emphasising each syllable, "the b-i-s-h-o-p is expecting you *today*."

I began to wonder if the bishop and God were synonymous. "Just tell the bishop," I said, "that I'll see him later in the week." The ominous silence was broken by the operator's "Three minutes up." With that, I hung up the receiver.

In 1946, one was permitted to take only $75 out of England. In Montreal's expensive metropolis my "allowance" was soon exhausted. After a brief sojourn and unable to afford another night's accommodation, I boarded the train for Toronto, arriving next morning at seven. I had a cup of coffee at the station restaurant and an hour later was on my way to the diocesan office. A heat wave had struck; the air was oppressive. How I longed for the early morning mists of the Wicklow hills. Quite literally, I hadn't a penny to my name, so to take a streetcar was out of the question. Following my brief encounter with the secretary over the long-distance telephone, I thought it might be foolhardy to take a taxi and arrive in style at the expense of the diocese.

Wearing a Harris tweed jacket, a pullover, heavy flannels, collar and tie, with a suitcase in each hand, I trundled along Yonge Street on a two-mile hike to Jarvis and Bloor, little realizing that I was treading the longest street in the world.

Wet and sticky and not, perhaps, in a particularly amiable frame of mind, I crossed the threshold into the cool of the office at Church House. All work ceased for a space as I was warmly greeted by the staff. Pleasantries concluded, I was ushered into the presence. Bishop Fleming was sitting at his desk. The moment I was announced, he stood up, crossed the floor and eagerly shook my hand, welcoming me to Canada and the Diocese of the Arctic in particular. If the bishop was horrified at my late arrival, he showed no evidence. He did not allude to it; nor did I.

Archibald Lang Fleming was the first Bishop of the Arctic. He was a canny Scot with the intriguing title, "Archibald The Arctic." Fleming was certainly one of the Anglican Church's super-salesmen. He was a man of great preaching ability and persuasive powers. Those talents, coupled with his considerable personal charm, brought many contributions to the diocesan purse during his preaching and lecture tours. The Arctic was a poor missionary area unable to support itself; it relied almost entirely upon outside assistance from various quarters, so the bishop's role in public relations was a vital one. He met the challenge with zeal and enthusiasm.

The annual supply ship for the eastern Arctic was not due to leave Montreal for a week or two, so I decided to spend a few days at an inn outside Toronto to escape the relentless heat. I had to borrow some money from the diocesan treasurer to meet the expenses. That, incidentally, was the only cash transaction between the diocese and me during my Arctic sojourn. This is not to imply that missionaries were expected to offer their services free of charge. What it does mean is that no money passed between missionary and diocese; our account was simply credited or debited on a monthly or quarterly basis.

To return to the haven of the inn: in what seemed the middle of the night, I got up to go to the bathroom. There were no facilities in my room, so I had to use the public bathroom just across the hallway. There was no air conditioning and I hadn't a stitch of clothing on. No one was abroad at the time so I left my door open and slipped in to the bathroom. While there, I heard a door slam and discovered to my horror that it was the door to my bedroom! I returned to the bathroom to ponder my predicament. Sitting on the edge of the bathtub, I scanned the area. There were no towels; not even a shower curtain. I knelt down and looked under the bathtub, the old four-legged variety, and my eyes caught sight of a small bath mat. Armed with the proverbial fig leaf, I ventured out in the direction of the reception desk in search of a key. Judging by the look on the attendant's face, he obviously thought that I had taken leave of my senses. One of life's embarrassing moments!

July 5th found me in Montreal again. I had now entered upon the final stage of my journey. To make perfectly sure that everything was in order, the bishop and I went to the office of the Hudson's Bay Company and reached it just before closing time.

As it turned out, it was most fortunate that we had. My name had not been included in the list of passengers due to sail on the annual supply ship, the RMS *Nascopie*. No sooner had that hurdle been overcome than the bishop discovered that his trunk of Arctic clothing had not arrived from Toronto. By the time this information reached him, the downtown stores had all closed, and we were due to set sail the following morning. Fortunately, shops in a subdivision remained open until nine o'clock, but the expedition was not very successful. Finally, the captain of the *Nascopie* produced a pair of green trousers - more suited to an Irish bishop!

We boarded the *Nascopie,* bound for Cartwright on the south coast of Labrador. The dock was crowded with people. Above the clamour, I could hear a clock strike ten as the ship moved slowly into the swiftly flowing waters of the St. Lawrence River. Once again, she was destined to visit the lonely outposts of the eastern Arctic. The cheering died away. Civilization became a memory. Icy fingers beckoned me - forerunners of isolation

The cruise down the St. Lawrence was exhilarating and the cool, refreshing breeze, after the insufferable heat of Toronto, was delightful. I began to live again.

Five days brought us to Cartwright on the south coast of Labrador. It is a little village made famous by the Grenfell Medical Mission. About the turn of the century, Sir Wilfred Grenfell founded a hospital at Cartwright. His exploits by dog team along the rugged coasts of Labrador are legion. As a result of his labours, the medical needs of the fishing communities were met. I spent three weeks here; a Newfoundland schooner had been detailed to take me on to Fort Chimo. At Cartwright I said farewell to the bishop. As a parting gift, he tucked an Eskimo grammar under my arm, and a cookbook from Mrs. Fleming.

Midnight, July 27th, I scrambled aboard the *J. H. Blackmore,* leaving my footmarks firmly imprinted on the greasy, rickety gangway on the last leg of my journey to Ungava Bay. I had experienced dirty ships before, but nothing to compare with this beauty. It had just returned from a sealing expedition. The deck was awash with gore, and the odd flipper could be seen here and there. My cabin, if one could call it that, was aft and was a regular thoroughfare. Anyone wishing to visit the stern of the ship inevitably passed through. The furnishings - I still recall a three-legged chair among the debris - were all homemade. My bunk was a masterpiece. In rough seas I had to jam my knees against the sides to stay put. In this berth I was expected to pass nine restful nights. Sheets and pillow cases were non-existent and the blanket decidedly on the hairy side.

One day I had occasion to visit the galley when the cook was in the throes of making bread. The kneading pan was a white, enamelled hand basin which had weathered many a storm. Most of the enamel had been chipped off. The cook was busily kneading the dough when I appeared on the scene. The heat was sufficient to drive one out of the kitchen, but I lingered to watch the operation. The dough was moistened, intermittently, from the beads of perspiration which adorned his brow. Presently, he picked up a lump of dough and began to finger it tenderly. I soon discovered that his false teeth, the "uppers," had fallen in. Undaunted, he retrieved them, picked them clean, replaced them and continued kneading. Suddenly I lost my appetite for bread. At mealtime, the crew was aghast at my abstinence. Imagine a meal without bread! But I kept my secret.

In all fairness, it must be recorded that the food on the whole was very good and in ample supply. The tablecloth, a permanent fixture, rivalled Jacob's coat of many colours. The crew, all Newfoundlanders, with unmistakably Irish voices, chatted incessantly and conversation ceased only at mealtime when chatter was replaced by chewing. In a sense, I felt quite at home again. They sounded as if they had just stepped off an Irish boat.

We made good time from Cartwright to a tiny place called Cutthroat Harbour, a two-day jaunt. A strong wind was now blowing and as ice could be seen in the distance, the skipper decided to drop anchor. We awoke the next morning to find our little haven packed with ice. A day's delay and we pushed on. The floating ice masses were so tightly packed that the distance covered was scarcely a mile. I had never seen anything quite like it. Most of the day was spent at the bow watching the ship weave and carve a passage. Often, she would mount a large ice pan, and unable to break it, slide back into the water. The skipper would give the order, "Astern." Another attempt would be made and, if successful, we would advance to battle the next. If not, the same performance would be repeated all over again. From time to time, we encountered small pans. With these, the icebreaker had little difficulty either pushing them aside or breaking them into fragments. Towards evening, the sea of ice lay behind us and all that could be seen now were clusters of pans, like tufts of cotton wool floating on a mill pond, so calm had the water become.

Unexpectedly we came upon a herd of walrus, for all the world like fat sausages lolling on pans in the sun. The first pair was snoozing peacefully so we were able to get within range. The skipper's son was the marksman. The first shot was on target. The female, which refused to leave her dead mate, was dropped with ease. As we approached the kill, the large male rolled off the ice into the water and sank. With the aid of a winch, the female was hauled on board. It would be decidedly "high" when we reached our destination. For the better part of two hours, we continued the hunt. Time was no object, but the wary mammals, now alerted, evaded us.

We ran into more ice accompanied by fog, until we reached Cape Chidley - Labrador's most northerly point. A gale forced us to drop anchor for 36 hours. Port Burwell, where we were scheduled to pick up a passenger, was our next port of call. We wasted little time; the place was deserted so we continued on our way.

The first week in August found us in Ungava Bay, and Fort Chimo loomed on the horizon. At the foot of the bay lies the Chimo River, called "Kuujjuaq," an Inuit word which means "big river." I was now on the home stretch. The skipper sounded the whistle, hoping that the Inuit pilot would be awaiting our arrival and was relieved when, shortly, a native boat could be seen making its way towards the schooner. Why a pilot, one might ask? The Kuujjuaq River, although two miles wide at the estuary, is a treacherous waterway and has claimed a number of lives. Shoals and reefs abound and the pilot, wise in these waters since his youth, was the logical person to take command. Having shaken hands with everyone on board, he commenced the task of bringing us safely to our journey's end. Fortunately, the tide was running in so there was no need for delay.

It was a 30-mile trip upriver. When some distance off, the pilot pointed out a small white speck on a piece of land jutting out into the river. He mumbled something about an igloo and I concluded that that was the mission house. As my eyes riveted on the "white speck," countless thoughts flashed through my mind. I was now looking at what was to become my Arctic home for the next three years. The schooner slowly moved upriver and the house began to take shape. Soon Fort Chimo lay before us.

The pilot brought us a little past the settlement, turned and stopped directly opposite it in the middle of the river. While we were still in the process of turning around, the Hudson's Bay Company boat *Meterk* drew near. There were two white men aboard: the outgoing Hudson's Bay post manager and the newly appointed manager of Fort McKenzie some 200 miles upriver (not to be confused with the mighty Mackenzie River which empties into the Beaufort Sea.) That same manager was to become, a year later, the post manager at Chimo. We introduced ourselves to the newcomers, presented them to the skipper and were on our way.

Baggage collected, we stepped into the motorboat and proceeded to the wharf above which, upon the rising ground, the entire population had assembled. The arrival of the annual supply ship was perhaps the most singular event in the Arctic year. It was a time when all families from near and far would converge on the settlement. This I knew, but drawing closer, I could scarcely believe my eyes. These people resembled the Inuit, but their clothes resembled white man's apparel. Where was the sealskin clothing one usually associated with them? Their sealskin boots were the sole clue to their identity. My eyes quickly scanned the men and women and came to rest on the words "Hudson's Bay Company, Established 1670" printed in large letters over the door of the store against which some of the women were leaning. Here was the answer. The Inuit had been given clothing in return for skins. Little did I realize then how much the white man's world had influenced these isolated people of the wastelands of the north.

I was the last to go ashore. Mounting the steps of the dock, I stood for a few minutes taking photographs while the remaining white people retired to the HBC house.

The gleaming white buildings with their red roofs - the Company's trademark in the Arctic - spruced up, no doubt, for the visit of the annual supply ship, formed a suitable backdrop. Close to the brow of the hill, in a commanding position, stood the HBC house - king of its tiny kingdom. At right angles, running down towards the river, were a series of buildings: store and warehouses, with a board sidewalk. In shape, the HBC compound resembled an inverted L. A little further north was a detachment of the Royal Canadian Mounted Police, and beyond that the mission house.

Return for a moment to the wharf. Through the viewfinder of my camera I could see an old Inuit woman waddling down the makeshift dock in my direction. And now, as if by evocation, I stand there again, seeing that weather-beaten, wrinkled but smiling face. The matriarch had come to inspect the new arrival. Her name was "Eeperautok" ("The Whip"). I later found that she was well named; her tongue could sting like a lash. She lived at the settlement throughout the year; her son was the assistant clerk and general handyman at the post. I came to know her well, and looking back through the vista of the years, I wonder if that first meeting was not slightly tinged with derision. Less than a decade had witnessed four missionaries at Fort Chimo. Was I to follow in quick succession?

The women stood by themselves on one side and the men on the other. Not a word was exchanged; all eyes were focused on us, the visitors. I moved forward to greet the people. Approaching the women,

I noticed their weathered complexion and high cheekbones. Their sleek blue-black hair was parted in the middle. The older women had plaits, caught back in a bun with pieces of string or ribbon. The teenagers preferred the flowing style, shoulder length. Long print dresses reached to within a span of the ankles. Tartan shawls, folded triangularly, rested on glossy crowns and draped over the shoulders with the corners tucked under folded arms. Irish gypsies, dwellers in caravans by country lanes, sprang to mind. All sported the traditional sealskin boots. Some mothers had children hitched onto their backs and a few held them in their arms. Others merely stood with arms clasped around their tummies. One uncoiled a flaccid hand and held it out. It could hardly have been called a handshake - my hand was pumped rather than clasped. It appeared as if they hadn't a worry in the world.

The teenage girls were extraordinarily shy and it was with some difficulty that I managed to grasp their hands at all. They kept looking down at their feet all the while with the shawls nearly covering their faces. The toddlers were the most amusing. The moment I made a move in their direction, they scampered off to their mother's side as fast as their little legs could carry them, howling for all they were worth, and clung to their mother's dress for dear life! Indeed most of them disappeared behind their mothers, feeling, no doubt, "out of sight, out of danger."

The Inuit men, in common with the women, were small of stature with faces wreathed in smiles. Their heads were shorn except for a small tuft in front. Like the women, they wore clothes from the store. They came forward to meet me and their shuffling gait was unmistakable; they leaned slightly forward with toes turned inward, slowly drawing one leg after the other. To use an athletic expression, "they sat on themselves."

Fort Chimo was rather different from what I had anticipated. I had visualized a small, permanent community of rough cabins. Such was not the case. True, it was small, but there were no cabins or any dwellings remotely resembling them. The inhabitants were tent dwellers. Houses would be an encumbrance. With notable exceptions, no families lived at the village. They brought their wares to the trading post, purchased the essential supplies and were off again.

The settlement overlooked the Kuujjuaq River and was protected from the rear by an arc of undulating hills which looked rather cold and uninviting. There were a few scrawny-looking spruce trees which bore the marks of many an icy blast. Tents dotted the landscape.

All the boat visitors had been invited to the HBC house as guests for tea, and the clerk was dispatched to find me. I was still busily greeting my new flock and had moved on to the south side of the settlement where the Indians had made camp. They had arrived from Fort McKenzie, a few hundred miles upriver, all prepared with their large cargo canoes to haul back supplies to their local trading post. Faintly aloof, they stood out sharply - an impressive band of Crees assembled in front of their teepees - some quite aristocratic in bearing. Almost immediately, I sensed an atmosphere of greater reserve with them than with the Inuit I had just met. My initial reaction was borne out during a canoe trip I made sometime later. By then I had grown accustomed to Inuit guides who on the whole were most helpful and looked after me well. The Crees possessed equal skills, but were less concerned with my comfort and welfare. In retrospect, I realize that I was never able, during those years, to establish any sort of personal relationship with them.

After tea, the post manager kindly escorted me to my quarters. The mission house stood by itself on a promontory. There was just the faintest trace of a trail through the maze of Arctic willows which opened out onto a veritable wilderness. Nature held sway; the hand of man had been absent these three years. Across the coarse rye grass, heads nodding in the breeze, stood the house, faintly haunted in appearance, a white wooden structure rising from the greenery.

Wading thigh deep through the meadow, we reached the back door. A sharp blow on the steel cleat and the rusted padlock yielded stubbornly, its reluctance echoing through the hollow building. The door, resenting the intrusion, opened unwillingly as we pushed. Within, all was gloomy and depressing, but thanks to the HBC people, clean and tidy.

Alone now with my thoughts, I wandered into the living room and sat on one of the twin monstrosities which served as armchairs but were quite comfortable withal. Alongside lay a box filled with wood and kindling. The receptacle no doubt had a history connected with it. In any event, in bold lettering and for all to see, was stamped "Hudson's Bay Best Procurable." From the potbelly stove rose a stovepipe which, when it reached the ceiling, turned and stretched across the room. It was suspended at intervals by wire straps. As a safety measure, wide strips of sheet metal had been nailed to the ceiling above the pipe. My roving eyes searched every corner of the room and my gaze came to rest on the floor. I wondered what the pattern on the faded linoleum had been. To try to piece it together would be more difficult than attempting a jigsaw puzzle.

Rising from the cotton-wool padded cushion, I began to explore the rest of the house. First, the bedroom. Here a large bed occupied two-thirds of the floor space. By the door stood a homemade washstand with a chipped enamel basin inset. I was sorely tempted to raise it to the ceiling with the toe of my shoe. Below reclined an equally battered water jug. Had I taken the vow of poverty? In the hall hung an antiquated sword with an ill-fitting sheath. An oak chest with impossible drawers was tucked under the stairway. The kitchen was equipped and well furnished: wood stove, table and chairs, numerous cupboards, and utensils galore. Adjoining, in common with all mission houses in the Arctic, was a special room where the Inuit and their families could visit at will and relax in comfort over a cup of tea and a biscuit. Such visits were to teach me much, not least the intricacies of the Inuit language.

Passing into the hall again, I commenced the ascent of the first of two flights of stairs. Aloft, five rooms, bare floors, a few bedsteads, table and chair and open shelves in a storeroom did not entice the new resident to linger. I retreated with all haste, took four steps in a stride, bolted through the doorway of the sun porch, cleared a broken-down picket fence and was on my way to the HBC house. I needed a loaf of bread for the morning.

Missionaries travelled far and wide, particularly during the winter months, so the house understandably lacked some of the amenities one normally associates with living quarters: running water, electricity and bathroom facilities. The outhouse, at a discreet distance, was hidden in the thicket. It listed heavily and was propped up with a beam and numerous boulders. Willows and long rough rye grass had found their way through the cracks. The wooden floor had rotted and the throne had suffered a similar fate. The door, ajar, hung by a rusty hinge. I was yet to experience the mosquito plague in the brief summer or the killer cold, harsh winds that would blast the frail structure and filter snow through the cracks in the long winter. Meditation would be short.

Following a fitful night's rest, I trotted over to The Bay to make enquiries about my "chore girls." Before leaving my native country, the secretary of the Diocese of the Arctic had sent me a detailed list of food, clothing and other necessities which would accompany me on the annual supply ship. Among the items were twelve "chore girls." Checking the list with the Irish secretary of the Society under whose auspices I had come to Canada, I asked, "What is a chore girl?" His reply was priceless. "You are a very lucky young man," he said. "These girls will keep house for you, one for each month of the year." Bearing this information in mind, I asked the post manager what had become of my chore girls. "Your what?" he asked. "My chore girls," I repeated, "the girls who are supposed to help me in the house." He began to laugh and went on to explain that a "chore girl" is a scouring pad used to clean pots and pans! I later discovered that the post manager, who always looked upon the Irish as a little odd to say the least, was no longer left in any doubt. This missionary must be quite mad!

Getting Adjusted

When I first arrived at Fort Chimo, the whole population looked very clean and presentable. Even the buildings had been tidied up and in some cases repainted in preparation for the arrival of the annual supply ship. However, as colder weather approached and washing became a problem, it was certainly more difficult to maintain the same standard. One often sees pictures of the Inuit in parkas heavily stained with seal oil, but living as they did under basic conditions, in tents or igloos, there was no alternative. They simply had not the facilities for keeping clean. It was also a problem for me at the mission house. There was no bathroom, and the Saturday night ritual meant hauling out the round galvanized tub and heating endless kettles of water on the wood stove. At best, bathing was an uncomfortable process. The tub, originally intended for laundry, also served as a protection for my feet when chopping wood. I used to stand in it as I wielded the axe, hoping the sides would deflect a careless blow.

Later on the trail, I soon learned that one had to be far from fastidious. I tried to make up for it by taking extra pains at home. From the very beginning, I changed my clothes every evening without fail before sitting down to dinner. Some of the locals found my custom rather amusing and hinted that I must have been brought up in very exalted surroundings. To me it was simply a matter of self-discipline and not a social nicety. I had seen and heard of too many people living alone in isolated communities allowing themselves to degenerate further and further. The term used in the Arctic was "bushed."

For the first time in my life I had to attend to household duties and do my own cooking. I was neither helpless nor stupid and it didn't take much skill to use a can opener, but as almost all our food came in cans one soon tired of the contents. One year I was so sick of meatballs that I decided to vary my diet and ordered hamburgers - not realizing that while the labels were different, the contents were the same! Eventually, after five years, I could turn out a reasonable meal - and I still bake bread.

It seemed to be a tradition in the Arctic that men made the bread - quite possibly because in the early days there were very few women. Certainly no help was available for me and my first efforts were hilarious. Those were the days of cake yeast and the overnight method. It was quite a problem to keep the dough sufficiently warm and after a number of failures I ended up by taking it to bed with me.

One of my early attempts was so dreadful that even the dogs, which normally would eat anything, turned up their noses at it. I remember once running out of yeast and resorting to Enos Fruit Salts as a leavening agent. It had the desired effect - in more ways than one.

During my second year, Morris, Bernice and Jerry Wright came to the HBC post at Fort Chimo. They were immensely kind and I had countless meals with them. They seemed to take pity on the Irish immigrant. Bernice was a wonderful cook and was able to produce delicious dinners from the same boring tins we all used. Actually, neither of the Wrights made bread; they had an Inuit girl to help in the house and she had learned to produce feather-like loaves.

Occasionally, I would entertain at the mission house and once had the audacity to bake rolls. I can still see Morris cutting one open and running his thumb over the not-too-delicate texture, very much in the way he graded fur on the counter in the store. Whatever his private reaction, he managed to get one down.

I never quite mastered the art of pastry making. I vaguely remembered hearing that a very hot oven was essential, but had no idea how hot was hot. I stoked the wood stove and the temperature was 500°F and rising when the pie went in. I carefully closed the kitchen door and went into the living room. The cookbook had suggested half an hour, but when I returned to check, the heat was unbearable and my masterpiece a cinder. Later attempts were a little better, but I always had trouble with shrinkage. As a remedy, I stuck the edge of the pastry to the pie plate with adhesive tape.

As one might imagine, there was not a great deal of social activity among the residents of Fort Chimo, mainly because there were so few of us - the post manager and his wife, the resident RCMP, and myself. We were a very congenial group and the Wrights were always endlessly kind and welcoming, but I tried not to impose upon them too frequently. One can outwear one's welcome all too easily in an isolated community and become a bit of a nuisance.

I was always keenly aware that their generosity far exceeded mine, partly because I spent most of the year travelling and partly because in the very early days particularly, as I have already mentioned, my cooking skills were rather limited. While I was never able to repay all that the HBC post managers did for me, it was possible to offer hospitality to others coming to the settlement. Max Dunbar and two of his assistants from McGill University spent a few summers with me at the mission house while taking part in a hydrographic survey. His work was somewhat exploratory in nature - the team was trying to locate fish and determine their source of food along the shores of Ungava Bay from Port Burwell to Payne Bay. The Fisheries Association of Canada had sponsored the project, chartering a plane from Montreal to transport the men and their heavy equipment. My house became their headquarters when they arrived in mid-June, but fortunately the enterprise took them away at intervals. I enjoyed their company immensely, but I was beginning to experience serious food shortages. Flour was the only staple I had in abundance and I really wondered if we might have to live on bread. The supply ship was not due until August.

Shortly after his arrival, Max offered to help me build a fish smoker near the river bank. It consisted of a largish hole dug in the ground where a fire was set alight. (Caribou moss provided the fuel.) Over the top of the hole a sheet of corrugated iron prevented the smoke from escaping into the open air. An eight-foot length of stove piping, buried in the earth, carried the smoke horizontally from the fire pot to an elbow pipe in the base of the chimney. The latter was built of bricks and mortar - walls two feet square and about two and a half feet in height. The fish were strung through the gills on the wire which spanned the opening at the very top. Food in the Arctic tended to be rather monotonous so the resulting harvest provided a welcome change from our usual diet and helped to ease my domestic concerns to some degree.

Several years later, when I had moved to Lake Harbour, I played host to Jim and Allie Houston on several occasions. At that time they were involved in Inuit handicrafts - both the soapstone carvings and the printmaking process. They were charming and delightful guests and while our paths seldom cross these days, we are still friends.

I tried to spend most mornings studying the Inuit language. It is beautiful and very complicated, but with the lilt and rhythm of Greek poetry. Like Greek, it has active, passive and middle voice; singular, dual and plural number. It has many words for which there are no English equivalents. There are, for example, anywhere from fifteen to twenty words for "snow." Prefixes, suffixes and infixes abound, which, if incorrectly placed, give an entirely different and often very amusing connotation.

On one occasion, a post manager with a reasonable grasp of Inuktitut dispensed some pills to an Inuk woman complaining of a headache. His advice, or so he thought, was to take a pill three times a day. Some time later she returned with the same complaint, but on this occasion the manager's wife, part Inuk and bilingual, was in the store. She questioned the patient about the prescription and started to laugh, asking her husband if he realized what he had said. It seemed that he had inadvertently told her to take a pill and turn around three times! This is an example of one of the many intricacies of the language.

During my first autumn, I spent most evenings studying as well. Fortunately for my eyesight, the mission house boasted excellent gasoline lamps which threw wonderful light and considerable heat. Evening study sometimes gave me a practical opportunity to improve my language skills when the Inuit dropped in to visit. They were free to come and go as they chose and I was pleased with both the practice and the companionship.

In 1946 the Inuit did not speak English. Of necessity, I had to conduct all services in the Inuit tongue. It was incredibly difficult at first and there was no one to help me.

The written language had been adapted by missionaries from the Cree Indian syllabic. When I had mastered the alphabet, I was able to write out the services phonetically, rather in the way a language dictionary shows pronunciation. After a few years I was reasonably comfortable, but real fluency in Inuktitut comes only after many years and I was not a linguist. I usually knew when I had made a mistake; my congregation was too polite to tell me, but they would laugh. The Inuit are very courteous and extremely reticent. One needs to know them a very long time before they will open up and share their thoughts and feelings.

Looking back, I now realize that I was learning two languages: Inuktitut and Canadian. The Wrights were frequently in stitches at what they considered my quaint expressions. After one of my first meals at the post house, I thanked them at the door and trying to compliment the hostess on her excellent cooking, I remarked, "I must say, Bernice, you are very homely." If Bernice's face showed bewilderment, Morris's was convulsed with mirth. I realized that I must have used the wrong word, but when they explained the difference between "homely" and "homey," I hastened to assure them that the latter had not been in my vocabulary.

On another occasion when, fortunately, I knew them much better, I really put my foot into it. Again, they had invited me to an evening meal. When I arrived, there were apologies that dinner was not quite ready. Knowing that the Wrights had turned one of the upstairs bedrooms into a table-tennis area, I remarked brightly to Bernice, "Let's go and have a knock-up to fill in the time." I thought Morris would explode, but I could not imagine what I had said to cause such a reaction. "Knock-up" was a term routinely used in Ireland to describe warming up before a game of tennis - batting the ball back and forth. When Morris had recovered his composure and wiped the tears from his eyes, he proceeded to educate me with a few well chosen words. I was mortified.

The obvious influence geography has on language reminded me of my mother's similar experience when she went to Ireland as a bride. The very first morning a voice called, "Shall I wet the tea, Ma'am?" My mother was completely mystified and looked imploringly at my father who had just come in for breakfast. He laughed and said, "She means infuse," and so began my mother's education in the local dialect.

Winter is a long season in the north. Evenings, which began in midafternoon, stretched interminably. There were few forms of recreation, no daily or weekly newspapers or magazines. We were all very dependent upon our own resources for entertainment and some people did not adjust very well.

I had a battery-operated radio, so was able at least to keep abreast of world events. Everyone in the settlement was an avid hockey fan and we regularly tuned in to "Hockey Night in Canada" with Foster Hewitt. "He shoots, he scores" became the highlight of the week. Many years later when I was the chaplain at Bishop Strachan School in Toronto, I had the great pleasure of meeting Foster Hewitt. His granddaughter was being baptized in the school chapel and that gave me the opportunity of saying how much I had enjoyed his broadcasts.

November was now upon us and the time had come to get my winter's supply of water. Apart from the Inuk clerk at the HBC, no Inuit lived at the settlement so I was dependent upon the arrival of the first dog team following freeze-up. Within a few days of the supply ship's departure, the community had broken camp and returned to their hunting grounds. It was towards the end of the month that the first sled appeared. I hired the Inuk and his team and we made the first trip, one of many, to the nearest suitable lake just over the hill. We were not going to draw water; our purpose was to draw ice.

Lashed onto the sled were an ice pick with a long handle, a pair of tongs, a gaff and an ice saw. The latter had large, jagged teeth and resembled a crosscut saw, but with one handle. The blade was tapered at the end. Arriving at the lake, we proceeded to hack out the first hole. The moment water was struck, a fountain of crystal-clear liquid gushed out. Johnny, an old hand at the job, stood to one side to avoid getting soaked. Four large holes, forming a rectangle, were chiselled. Inserting the saw in one, we began the operation. Using a crosscut for wood is child's play compared with sawing ice. Cutting through a solid mass requires strength and the technique of an expert. To control a long, flexible blade is no mean feat. As the winter approaches, the further one goes out onto a lake the thicker the ice becomes. It can run to a depth of three feet, so it is important to get one's supply in good time.

Having cut a block, the problem was to extricate it. Using the gaff, Johnny was able to lift one end out of the water, spike it with the tongs and haul it onto the ice. With a number of blocks safely landed, we began to load the sled. The team consisted of eight dogs, so the total weight could not exceed 750 pounds. Roughly speaking, a dog is capable of pulling 90 pounds. However, on this occasion the snow was deep and the going slow so we had to make a number of trips. In fact, it took the greater part of two days to complete the job.

Back at the mission house, we unloaded the sled and dumped the first load into an old fifty-gallon oil drum which stood in a corner of the kitchen. It was the only receptacle available. The remainder was neatly stacked by the back door. The cost of the work involved? Johnny was very reluctant to accept anything. I pressed a few plugs of tobacco into his hand. His face was the picture of contentment

Just as ice cutting was a yearly operation, so was the task of re-ordering the food supply for the next year to arrive on the annual supply ship in July or August.

In early winter the shelves were well stocked, but as the mail came in and went out by plane only four times a year at best, one had to plan six months ahead. In the beginning, a great deal of guesswork was necessary and there were inevitable mistakes. After a year or two of trial and error, I was able to forecast my needs reasonably accurately.

We enjoyed fresh food only in the brief time immediately following the supply ship's annual visit. It was wonderful to have such luxuries as fresh meat and potatoes. Fruit and vegetables were too fragile to ship so we learned to do without these delicacies.

All supplies had to be carefully checked against the original order list and discrepancies reported to the diocesan office. The Inuit were very considerate about humping my crates from the dock to the mission house, just as they had carried all my belongings when I first arrived. It was a kindness I did not reward personally, but suspect that the HBC, which hired the community at ship time for unloading purposes, probably included my things with theirs. I always found the Company extremely generous and often felt that the missionaries would not have survived very comfortably without it.

Christmas Day, 1946

As part of the North American defence system, an American-manned air base had been established about five miles upriver from Chimo. The staff was small and we saw them only occasionally, although we did sometimes benefit from their generosity. The post exchange (PX) was a treasure trove with very reasonable prices, but sadly none of us had much money to spend. After considerable thought, I finally splurged $90 - a fortune, considering my salary - on a Retina 2, 35 mm camera, which would in time provide all my Arctic slides. It proved to be an excellent investment and is still in use. The bishop was not so enthusiastic. As we seldom had cash, the cost had to be charged against my account at the diocesan office in Toronto, so of course any purchases could be subject to comments and sometimes were. Missionaries often found it understandably difficult to live within their means and there was frequently some concern about overdrafts and possible non-repayment. The Church budget was minimal and did not allow for any extravagance.

Christmas time was an ideal occasion for a community celebration. We were all far from home and for three of us at Chimo it was our first Christmas in the Arctic. I rose early and celebrated Holy Communion at St. Stephen's Church at eight o'clock, using a service in Inuit syllabics for the first time. My congregation had been away on their hunting grounds during the autumn, so this was really my initial attempt in conducting worship in their language. There were seventy-five communicants. A second service followed at nine-thirty in English for the white residents - five in all. We said Morning Prayer at eleven - again a full church.

During the afternoon I helped Frank Hynes, the post manager, to carry out a huge bag full of tobacco, sweets, chocolates, and other treats for a "scramble" which the Inuit thoroughly enjoyed. Everyone - men, women and children - joined in. It was great fun watching them fall over one another in search of what had been tossed up in the air. I think we derived as much pleasure watching it as they did taking part. The little ones simply loved anything of this nature. One elderly woman bent down and was about to pick up a bar of chocolate which had fallen at her feet when suddenly a small child standing behind her dived in between her legs and snatched the candy. The little fellow got more than he had bargained for as she fell forward and landed on him!

Just before the bag was empty, George Mackay, the RCMP, came along with extra food and I went to collect a bucket full of biscuits and sweets. The HBC provided boxes of cornflakes. As a final effort, the game continued at the mission house for more cornflakes, puffed rice and beef fat. I also distributed a few boxes of cereal to the older women who had not been successful in the scramble.

The remainder of the afternoon was spent at the HBC house in anticipation of our Christmas feast. The air base had provided turkey, sweet potatoes and ice cream. George had volunteered as cook and he certainly excelled himself. However, he had a habit of wearing mukluks in the house and while taking the turkey out of the oven his foot slipped, perhaps on a bit of grease, and he fell full length on the floor. I had walked into the kitchen to see how our cook was getting along, and found him covered from head to foot with gravy. The turkey, little affected by the fall, lay a few feet away on the floor. The roaster, turned upside down, was under the table beside the dining-room door. Its lid was actually in the dining room. George's face was a combination of disgust and frustration. The thought of losing such good gravy was too much for him! As he began to collect in a saucer what was left, I said, "George, you're not going to use that *now*...." There was no reply.

Before sitting down to the table, he had to run over to his house and change every stitch of clothing. When the meal was over, we remained seated because, having eaten so much, we were quite unable to move. Everyone congratulated George on his fine effort. He turned to me and asked if I had enjoyed his specialty - the gravy.

I just smiled.

Trading at the Post

The first dog team appeared the second week in December when the ice had formed on the river and a blanket of snow covered the landscape. The Hudson's Bay Company had long been trading with the Inuit. In the mid-1940s the pattern was very much the same: fox and seal skins, marten and beaver in exchange for tea, tobacco, flour and clothing - and usually in that order. Join me in the store and see a unique system of trading.

Stores are unheated and business is reasonably brisk. The Company is not trying to save money; the purpose is to discourage loitering. The temperature within the frame building is about -25°F Outside it hovers around the -30°F mark.

The first contingent arrives. In this patriarchal society, the man leads the way, followed by his wife and children. They cross the threshold, stamping their feet. The creaking floorboards strongly resent the added weight. The family doff their sealskin mitts; placing the palms of their hands together, they ease off the mitts with their fingers, then tuck the mitts under an arm. Soon, the store is well filled and the air thick and foggy. The temperature rises a few degrees and the heavy smell of cigarette smoke and seal oil pervades.

The first to arrive is not necessarily the first to be served. The Inuit love to visit and gossip, and this may well be the first meeting of the clan since the parting of the ways in the fall.

On the long counter the Inuk displays his wares, chiefly fox furs. Each skin is carefully examined. Every post manager has served his apprenticeship and is well schooled in this aspect of the fur trade. Taking a fox skin (the best pelts are on the top) from the pile, he lays it on the counter with the fur uppermost. Placing one hand on the head and taking the rump in the other, he shakes the head several times. This causes the fur to stand erect so he can see the guard hairs at a glance. The next step will determine the quality or "body" of the fur.

With the pelt still on the counter, he holds the tail and runs the palm of his hand slowly towards the head. This is repeated several times. Now comes the moment of truth: the price is established. The Inuk accepts the figure without question.

The post manager places on the counter a set of tokens corresponding to the value of the fur. Note the word "tokens." Barter, rather than a cash economy, is the rule of the day. Dollar bills and currency are a rare commodity. Suppose a pelt is worth $10.50. The trader places ten aluminum tokens - somewhat larger than an English penny - and a 50-cent token, smaller in size to avoid confusion, on the counter. Although $1.00 and $.50, respectively, are clearly marked, the Inuk is guided by size rather than by designation. All the while his wife is in the background. She now comes forward to assist her husband in making the necessary choice of provisions. Behind the counter are row upon row of shelves, filled to overflowing, which simplifies the purchase of the goods considerably. The index finger works overtime.

In 1947 at Fort Chimo the Hudson's Bay factor was Morris Wright. He had been trained in Indian country, notably the Chibougamou and Misstassini areas, and this was his first posting in the Arctic. Understandably, his knowledge of the language was extremely limited. His five-year-old son, Jerry, soon came to the rescue. Like all children, he quickly picked up the local dialect and in a matter of months was able to get by. His father was both delighted and relieved and promptly made him the official interpreter.

Fox fur is predominant in the Ungava district and Fort Chimo was no exception. I have seen many beautiful skins, but the most exotic is the blue fox. It is a variation of the white and runs one in a hundred. A matched pair of blues is both rare and costly. The white fox, usually called the Arctic fox, is the smallest of the species and does not interbreed with the red. It spends its entire life on the open tundra and lemmings are its main source of food. The red fox, on the other hand, lives within the tree line; it can produce a silver and a cross fox in the same litter. It is even possible for a red vixen to give birth to three cubs, one red, one silver and the third a cross. The latter is perhaps least well known. It is intermediate between red and silver.

Return to the store for a moment. To my knowledge, the Hudson's Bay Company in the Arctic took into consideration the needs of their customers, and the Inuit welfare was of considerable concern to them. In my experience the Inuit were well treated by the Hudson's Bay Company. Occasionally, there was the story of the odd trader who made an extra dollar or two at the expense of an Inuk, but by and large the Inuit were given a fair shake.

The HBC was certainly not present in the north for any reasons of social concern; quite obviously the motive was profit. However, I personally did not see any evidence of exploitation or ill treatment. The post managers whom I knew showed great concern for the people of the Arctic as a whole. Every post was well equipped with medical supplies and most managers were in charge of the dispensary. Only a few settlements had trained medical assistance.

Independent traders - and there have been a number of them from time to time - were often at odds with the Hudson's Bay Company. The larger Company could afford to charge a little less for supplies than the free-lancer. With its great resources it could stand by the Inuk and his family in bad times and good. The Inuit could always rely on the HBC to help them in time of need. Smaller operations had not the means to offer such support and their tenure in the north was not always so reliable nor of long standing. The HBC continued a solid lifeline. The Inuit were not the only recipients of a post manager's consideration. I was frequently housed and fed by many of them during my travels and their kindness made a somewhat spartan life more bearable.

One used to hear stories about the cost of rifles when they were first introduced into the north country. The Inuk piled his skins one on top of the other and the trader would rest the butt of a rifle on the counter beside them. When the topmost pelt reached the tip of the barrel, that would determine the price. It is an interesting story, but I have never met anyone who could vouch for its authenticity.

Travelling in the Bush Country

It was fortunate that ever since my arrival in the Arctic, I had had an overwhelming desire to ride the trail, explore the land and see the Inuit and wildlife in their natural surroundings. I soon realized that my congregation was a very scattered one and if I were to know my people at all and be of any real help to them, I must go out to their camps. Sharing their lives, even on a small scale, would promote understanding and possibly forge some bond between us.

Before the first snows dusted the landscape and the hunters and their families had taken off for winter quarters, through an interpreter I made arrangements with an Inuk to take me to George River, which is about 150 miles northeast of Fort Chimo. Although times and dates mean little to these northern inhabitants, I had made it abundantly clear to the guide that I expected to be on my way on January 14th, by which time winter travelling would be reasonably favourable.

The first day of the new year dawned grey and gloomy with a haze hanging over the river. Such weather, with intermittent snow flurries, was to continue for the greater part of the month.

The day of departure arrived, but there was no sign of my team. January 15th and 16th came and went and I was still patiently waiting. How frustrating! What could have happened? Perhaps there had been an accident - one could imagine all kinds of misfortune - or my guide had mistaken the day. Worse still, had he forgotten all about our agreement?

Four days behind schedule, I could see a team in the distance picking its way across the river ice. As it came within striking distance of the settlement, I was horrified to see only five dogs, scrawny and in a poor physical state. Obviously, the pickings in the summer and fall, when the huskies spend their days scavenging, had been scanty. Ten dogs would be a full complement for this woodland trip where the snow is deep and the heavily laden sled would sink a foot or more in the "maowyuk" (deep snow). I had visions of having to find more than half the team myself. To make matters worse, the lead dog, the most important and valuable of the pack, was lame. More gloom was to follow. The sled was too short and not at all practicable for long-distance travel. My guide had brought nothing save a makeshift stove and pipes, a kettle, and a few handfuls of tea in a battered saucepan. He had neither polar bear nor caribou skins for the floor of the tent, no food of any kind, no tent or sleeping bag. He lived for the most part at an Inuit camp about 50 miles upriver and had always arranged his itinerary in such a way that he reached another camp each evening. There he would be fed and watered and supplied with food for the next day's journey at someone else's expense. The Inuit are most kind and generous and would never contemplate for a moment seeing one of their own, or anyone else for that matter, starve so long as there was something to eat. I could not imagine how any individual in his right mind could even contemplate a journey under such circumstances. Perhaps he thought that I, as missionary-in-charge at Chimo, was a miracle worker.

Every year, the diocesan office dispatched bales of clothing to all mission stations in the eastern Arctic. These bales were stuffed with all kinds of gear, clothing and bedding, and the missionaries were responsible for seeing that this was fairly distributed among the Inuit people, particularly the needy. All were most appreciative. And how pleased were we, as missionaries, to be able to help. I was certainly grateful to the members of the Women's Auxiliary - Anglican Church Women as they are known today - for their untiring efforts on behalf of the Inuit: the countless hours spent sewing, knitting and mending articles of clothing. No sooner had the bales been sent off than they set to work in preparation for the following year's shipment.

My guide, Moses, had no suitable clothing for the trip ahead, so I looked in one of the remaining bales. By chance, there was a comforter as well as shirts, underwear, socks and Harris tweed trousers. He was the recipient of all these and I began to feel that he had fared rather well. For some odd reason, and totally out of character for an Inuk, he was not satisfied. He saw a new pair of shoes on the floor and promptly requested them for his wife. Exasperated, I said that he could have them for $20. There were no further demands.

Clothes for the Journey

I had envisaged intrepid Arctic travellers looking like stuffed mummies when exposed to subzero weather. Nothing could be further from the truth. To sit idly on a sled all day long, admiring the view, would spell disaster. It is essential to jump off from time to time and jog or walk to keep the circulation going. This is not so easy as it might sound. Too much exercise could lead to problems. Overexertion can cause perspiration and this, in turn, will freeze when one resumes a seat on the sled. One has to steer a middle course and hope for the best. Experience is the only teacher.

My clothing was simple, practical and nonbulky. Long johns are essential and, preferably, on the large side. Tight underwear is a great mistake. Indeed, anything too snug is to be avoided. A viyella shirt, a pair of worsted trousers and a turtleneck sweater were all worn.

Footwear consisted of long, heavy woollen stockings and duffel socks. The socks were a coarse woollen fabric with a thick nap, extending just below the knee, with a cuff at the top. Sealskin boots were of two kinds: one for winter and one for spring and summer use. The latter were watertight despite the fact that they were sewn together with needle and caribou sinew. The margins were overlapped, not sewn edge to edge, similar to the way in which the edges of a coat are overlapped when buttoned up. They were a murky brown with all the fur removed. The winter boots, on the other hand, had cream-coloured feet, fur scraped off with an ulu, but the oil, for warmth, had not been extracted. They smelled to high heaven! The fur was left on the legs, with a drawstring on top to prevent the snow from getting in. A second pair of trousers, legs at half-mast, were made from drill to help break the wind. Rickrack adorned the lower part of the leg. It served no useful purpose, but the seamstress assured me that it "finished them off." A pair of duffel and sealskin mitts, a white fox fur parka - the gift of the bishop - and a tuque crowned the attire.

Food for the Trail

Food for the trail was quite a problem and, as it turned out, a disaster. Normally, one could get an idea from the post manager or the RCMP, but both were new arrivals in Chimo and were as ignorant as I. I filled a crate with cans of various meats and vegetables and threw in a few tins of butter and jam. Hardtack biscuits, quantities of scones, tea and sugar completed the menu.

Thanks to The Bay and the RCMP, I was able to borrow six dogs, one of them a leader, and a sled. The day of departure arrived. The dogs were tethered to a rock while the sled was being loaded. It was a slow and exacting job and Moses was painfully methodical. The grub box, with most of our food, was foremost. It had a sliding door, at an angle of about 45 degrees, and could be opened without unlashing the load. The handle, of whalebone, was fastened to the top of the box. It served as a steering wheel and was essential for keeping the sled on course. Should it snap, a few strands of looped sealskin line could serve the purpose.

Alongside the grub box, and extending almost the full length of the sledge, was the dog food. The seal meat had been cut up into chunks, dumped into sacks or skin bags and placed on the crossbars, end to end. Each bag weighed about 50 pounds. The length of the trip determined the quantity. There was sufficient room at the rear for the crate of tinned supplies, stove and pipes, primus stove and coal oil. The next layer took care of our sleeping bags and dunnage bags, with extra clothing and the willow mats. Caribou and polar bear skins were draped over the load and fastened securely with sealskin line. Rifles, for ready use, were lashed on top. My cameras, in a cotton wool padded bag, were similarly attached. Last, but by no means least, the black tea kettle. The Inuit could scarcely survive without one.

It was a red-letter day in the life of the community to see a team take off on a journey, and they all joined in the fun. There had been a small gathering of the clan immediately after freeze-up. The sled was loaded, the dogs giving tongue and straining at the traces, the children in friendly combat clambering aboard, the less fortunate precariously perched with one foot on the outer rim of a crossbar and the other dangling in the air, the elderly cheering and giving last minute instructions. Moses gave the order: "Attai" ("Go!") The sledge didn't budge; it was firmly rooted in a deep, white mound. Moses jumped off, rocked the sled, cracked the whip, and we were away in a cloud of snow. Ecstasy, however, was short lived.

The dogs made a beeline for the river. Reaching rough shore ice, the team came to an abrupt halt; again the sled was deeply wedged, this time between hummocks of ice. The impact sent the passengers flying in all directions. No one was injured. Laughing, the children picked themselves up and thought it all a great joke. Moses was not amused. Fortunately, the runners escaped unscathed. The bystanders came to the rescue. The dogs were unhitched and axes used to dislodge the sled. Inch by inch, pushing, pulling, heaving, huffing and puffing, we guided it onto the river, rehitched the dogs and we were on our way again - a little more subdued, perhaps. It was rather embarrassing to come to grief in full view of the settlement. I was beginning to question the experience of my so-called guide.

We proceeded downriver for a number of miles, found a suitable opening in the shore ice and began the ascent of the riverbank. Reaching the top, we glided along one of the many lakes and both of us sat on the sled and began to relax. The temperature was -40°F. When well under way, the dogs settling down to a steady pace, I asked in halting Inuktitut - Moses couldn't speak a word of English - "How long will the trip take us?" His reply was typical and not wholly unexpected: "Ah-tuke," which means "I have no idea." How extraordinary, I thought. This man had made the trip to George River on numerous occasions, but hadn't the foggiest notion how many days it would involve. My knowledge of the language was so limited at the time that I was unable to query him further so let the matter drop. I was to discover many weeks later that a number of factors have to be taken into consideration: weather, travelling conditions and the physical state of the dogs, all of which have a direct bearing on the expedition.

At the beginning of winter when the snow is very soft and deep, ten miles a day is a fair distance. Conversely, in the spring, when the howling gales of winter have packed the snow so hard that one could not make the slightest impression on it with the heel of a mukluk, it is possible to canter along and cover anything up to 80 miles a day. At that time of year, the sun rises early and sets late. An 18-hour day is not unusual.

To return to my initial question. The Inuit never think in terms of hours, days or even weeks. "Sleeps" is their yardstick. Had I asked him, "How many sleeps to George River?" he might still have said, "Ah-tuke." If pressed for a more precise answer, he would probably have said,

"Four or five," but would have immediately qualified it by adding "im-ah-ha." The word means "maybe." The Inuit are very reluctant to commit themselves.

The going continued fair and we decided the time had come for a mug-up: tea and hardtack biscuits. Kindling was abundant. We had little difficulty getting a fire going. A Y-shaped stake was driven into the ground and a kettle hung on it. Meanwhile, the sled was upturned, runners planed and re-iced. This is a daily chore. If travelling conditions are poor, it may be done three or four times.

Tea was poured into chipped enamel mugs - enough to put anyone off - and we attacked the hardtack biscuits (appropriately named - dunking was the only solution.) Little time was wasted. Mugs were rinsed out with snow, dumped in the grub box, the sled was righted and we trudged along. Putting on a pair of bear-paw snowshoes, the type worn in my area, I began to break trail ahead of the dogs. The western Arctic Inuk favours the raven's foot style. Those snowshoes are considerably longer, narrower and turned up at the toe.

There is a decided art to snowshoeing. The bear-paw snowshoes are so wide it is impossible to walk normally in them. The solution is to swing the legs in an outward, circular motion from the hips. In this way, there is little danger of overlapping and falling headlong into the snow. I had made many trial runs on snowshoes and thought that I was reasonably proficient, but a few hours' tramping through the dense woods was more tiring than expected. Unable to proceed further, I sat down on a tree stump and awaited the team.

Travelling in the bush country can be very confusing. Surrounded by tall, stately spruce trees, one can go in circles without realizing it, but I had read somewhere that moss grows on the north side of a tree. That was my guide. Half an hour passed and I began to wonder if I was off course. I wasn't too concerned; the team would eventually track me down. I cannot say that I really enjoyed the experience. Hemmed in on all sides, I felt claustrophobic. Arctic hare and ptarmigan tracks were all over the snow. Ptarmigan are members of the grouse family. This particular species was spruce ptarmigan and, unlike their willow and rock cousins, retain their partridgelike plumage all year. As I sat patiently waiting, they perched on spruce boughs within easy range, but my rifle was on the sled. Eventually, Moses appeared. He had bagged a brace on the way. Another mug-up, the runners were re-iced and we pushed on. As I was fastening the thong of the snowshoes around my ankles, Moses said, "Keep the team in view at all times." Rather subtle, I thought.

Resuming the trek, I began to appreciate "Nature's Cathedral." Trees here and there had been felled, which indicated that countless teams had passed this way for generations. Here in the depth of the forest, one could see the advantage of harnessing the dogs in a fan-hitch. In the open, the dogs could run spread out (as a fan). Between the trees, the dogs ploughed their way single file (the fan now closed) with the more powerful in front and the weaker and less seasoned closer to the sled.

It was early afternoon and in the gathering gloom we decided to call it a day. In the heart of the woodlands, miles from anywhere, we pitched tent. Travelling tents were small and could be erected with little difficulty. The supporting poles were cut on the spot and inserted. The required number of pegs were notched, pointed and driven into the ground. Tent in place, small spruce boughs were needed to "brush" the floor. While I was busy laying the floor, Moses chopped wood into suitable lengths for the stove, and dropped them by the door. These were neatly stacked inside. The sacks of seal meat were dragged in which helped to anchor the boughs. Next came the grub box and the small camp stove. It stood on four stakes, about a foot from the floor, with its pipes threaded through a circular hole in the ceiling of the tent. Sheeting iron was wrapped around the perimeter as a precautionary measure. The kindling was damp so it was sprinkled with coal oil to get the fire going. There was a solid bed of glowing embers before the logs were added. In no time we had a roaring fire. We soon discovered, however, that something was missing: the flat, circular sheets of metal for covering the openings on the top of the stove. Sparks were flying and flames, leaping up, threatened to burn the tent. Moses managed to unearth a flat stone to cover one hole. We stuck the kettle over the other. Coal oil and primus stove were stashed outside. Finally, polar bear and caribou skins were brought in.

All the while, the dogs were still hitched to the sled. The main trace, or bridle, was unbuttoned and promptly attached to a tree. One has to be prepared for any emergency. Normally, after a hard day's work, huskies are glad to curl up in the snow and rest, but prowling wildlife could alter things drastically. Two tripods, about 15 feet apart, were erected and the sled hoisted on top. It was secured with the long lash of the whip.

It was now time to feed the dogs. Great care is taken to make sure that each animal gets an equal amount of seal meat: three pounds each per night, fed individually. To empty a sack on the snow and let the dogs go to it would mean that several would go hungry. There is a pecking order in every team and the boss dog would certainly devour more than his fair share. Huskies replete, the harness and traces were neatly coiled, tied together and fastened onto the sled. The snowshoes and willow mats were also hung up out of danger's reach. Chores finished, we now began to prepare the evening meal.

Deep within the woods with no lake nearby, we had to settle for snow water. Making tea from the latter is a culinary challenge. If snow is dumped into a kettle and placed on the stove, the resulting water will have a metallic taste; the water will be "singed." The trick is to put the snow into a cold kettle, heat it gradually, shaking constantly until there is an adequate supply of water. When the pot was well filled, we added the tea. It was boiled for several minutes, removed from the stove, another handful of tea was added for good measure and topped off with a mug full of snow. As an Irishman, I enjoy strong tea, but this was a pretty ghastly brew!

My first trip was not without its difficulties. The next problem taxed the ingenuity of even an Inuk. On reflection, I realize I should have made greater preparations for the trip beforehand. In assuming that my guide would have seen to all the equipment, I had taken too much for granted. By nightfall, the canned goods were solidly frozen and neither of us had a can opener or penknife. Moses bashed a tin of meat with the axe and pried it open. We shared the contents. So much effort was involved that we decided not to attack another. Meanwhile, Moses prepared the ptarmigan. They were skinned rather than plucked, feathers and all, and put on the stove in the kettle to boil. They were very tasty. Certainly Moses devoured his with relish, dipping each morsel into a small pail of rancid seal oil. A loud belch of satisfaction accompanied each bite. I enjoy grouse which is well hung, green in fact, but this putrid seal fat nearly blew me out of the tent. Moses crushed the bones and extracted the marrow. Nothing was wasted - not even the intestines.

The skins, which served as groundsheets, were spread on the spruce floor, sleeping bags were unrolled and we crawled in for the night. At some ungodly hour, long before daybreak, Moses lighted the stove, put on the kettle and we had breakfast. While I was munching a scone, Moses was planing and icing the runners. It took the best part of an hour to lash our goods onto the sled and hitch up the dogs. We were thinking of caching the crate of tinned goods and picking it up on the return journey, but decided otherwise. Putting on snowshoes and grabbing my rifle, I began to break trail again. In short order, the team caught up with me. A good night's rest and food to boot had made all the difference in our rate of progress.

The snow lay deep and heavy and walking was the only possible order of the day. A few mug-ups and many hours slogging brought us to an Inuit campsite.

Daisy's Camp

We pulled in to Daisy's camp before the sun made its brief appearance of the day. There were six tents in all. Our arrival was not totally unexpected; the Inuit equivalent of jungle drums had been at work. While Moses was unlashing the sled, I made the rounds. The men were away hunting or tending their traplines, but the women welcomed me enthusiastically and I shook hands with everyone. Plied with tea and bannock in each tent, I floated back to Daisy's in time for supper.

Before describing the tent and furnishings, let me say a word about Daisy. She was the perfect hostess and knew how to look after the comforts of a white guest. She had worked a number of years for several HBC factors and their wives so could understand English, but in the presence of her own people she refused to utter a word. She had a ten-year-old daughter and lived with her mother, Jeannie, and brother, Johnny. The latter had also served an apprenticeship with the Company. He, too, had a fair grasp of English, but was equally reticent. There did not appear to be a "Mr. Daisy." The fact that I decided to stay here for two nights might well have caused raised eyebrows in civilization, but there was really no alternative.

The tent floor was brushed with spruce branches, intertwined to keep them in place. Wide canvas strips covered the boughs. These strips catch all the bits and pieces and can be removed from time to time and shaken out-of-doors. To one side was the stove. It, too, was rectangular in shape - circular heaters are the exception - and stood on four steel pipes which had been driven into the ground. Daisy's particular shelter was a permanent fixture and housed the family for twelve months of the year. The main bunk was directly opposite the door. It was an elaborate structure and reminiscent of a four-poster bed. Four substantial poles had been set in place. The construction began at ground level. All the tiers were dovetailed at each post and chinked with a mixture of mud and moss. The height of the finished masterpiece was about three feet. The cavity was filled with tender spruce branches. The "bedspring" was overlaid with skins and threadbare clothing - anything, in fact, which might add to the comfort. This was, without doubt, the most pleasant bunk in which I had ever slept in the Arctic. And that includes the mission house.

Two more bunks, not quite so large but similarly built, ran along the side walls. At the foot of each bunk was a box with the top covered in print fabric. Here meals were served. At last, something could be done about the canned supplies.

Daisy put some tins in a saucepan of water and heated them. When they had thawed sufficiently, she removed them from the water, emptied the contents into another pot and placed it on the stove to cook. In short order, we had a hot meal which we all enjoyed. A bannock, at that time a staple of the Inuit diet, was being prepared as a second course. The frying pan was swimming in seal fat as the unleavened cake was dropped in. It was all that I could do to eat it, but it was more palatable hot than cold. We capped off the meal with biscuits and the inevitable tea.

Before retiring for the night, I paid a visit to another large tent. My movements had been watched; families began to pour in. Someone had a small piano accordion which accompanied songs, religious and secular. We ended with a service and the gathering dispersed when I left for Daisy's tent at nine-thirty.

The dishes had been washed and my sleeping bag was unrolled and turned down. When I removed my mukluks, Daisy turned them inside out and began to chew them. They were damp with perspiration. Notwithstanding, she softened each boot, mended a hole in one and hung them up for the night. Jeannie helped with the chores, but drew the line at chewing the skins. This had been her role for many years, but her teeth were now worn down close to the gums. Duffel socks and mitts were also hung up to dry.

Bedtime arrived. Who would make the first move? Not I. "Ladies first" was my motto. Uninhibited, drawstrings on mukluks untied, boots kicked off, dresses shed, the girls jumped into their sacks. Equally unruffled, I stripped to my long johns and crawled into mine. Jeannie slept under an eiderdown quilt. Hers was genuine and not the synthetic kind. Daisy and her daughter had Hudson's Bay four-point blankets.

The stove, for my benefit, no doubt, had been banked to last most of the night.

I awoke to a tapping noise above my head. There had been a heavy snowfall and Jeannie was trying to clear the sagging roof. It had been so comfortable last night I was reluctant to get up and face the elements. The snow had ceased by noon when I ventured out. In need of exercise, I walked to a nearby river which enters Ungava Bay. On my way, I came upon several women jigging for fish through the ice. Using an ice chisel with a long handle, they had chopped a circular hole in the ice. A homemade scoop with a handle was used periodically to keep the hole free of fragments. Fishing rods were not used. A piece of string attached to a short stick held a weighted hook and a strip or two of coloured wool. Some had no hooks at all, just a weighted line with ribbon. The jigging motion attracted the fish. Each fisherwoman had a spear in one hand in readiness to spike the catch the moment it appeared. The spear was not unlike Britannia's trident.

We were about to prepare the evening meal when we heard a great commotion outside the tent: Johnny had returned from the hunt with three beautiful lake trout, the largest of which was about three feet in length. In true Inuit fashion, these became common property; the whole camp shared in the feast, myself included. For those who enjoy the out-of-doors, nothing is so delicious as fresh fish cooked over a campfire. Earlier in the season, Johnny had set some nets in the lake. This was his fifth harvest.

Next morning, very reluctantly, we set off to the cheers and farewells of the community. Snowshoes were again essential; the heavy snowfall had made conditions far from ideal. It was a pleasant surprise, and relieved the monotony somewhat, to run into another team about midday. We halted for a third mug-up. Any excuse for a rest, but it was welcome nevertheless. Moses was able to enquire about travelling conditions. Luck was on our side; the other driver had come from George River and was returning to the vicinity of Fort Chimo. We had visions of a broken trail all the way, but another day's snowfall would soon put an end to our dreams. I noticed white fox on his sled, an indication that we were getting close to the barren lands. The white fox lives its entire life on the open tundra. While the Inuit were chatting away and getting caught up on the latest gossip, I untangled the traces.

Moving on, we soon found ourselves in the barren lands. How aptly they are named. They look as if some mighty hand had scattered rocks and boulders indiscriminately across their face. The tundra is a treeless, rolling wasteland. An American pilot who had flown in to Baffin Island on a mercy mission, once remarked to me, "God must have created this place on the sixth day." Falling for it, I had asked, "Why?" The answer: "He was obviously very tired at the time."

Despite the snowfall, the going improved considerably, a sharp contrast between bush-country and barren-land travelling. We crossed a series of lakes and were able to ride the sled and relax. The sun, a ball of fire, sank into oblivion at two-thirty in the afternoon, so we camped. Normally in the barren lands, one sleeps in an igloo, but Moses had never built one in his life. This is not unusual; the bush country Inuk lived in tents throughout the year. His sallies into the wastelands were infrequent and of short duration. (In the same way, the barren-land Inuk could not walk in snowshoes and did not possess a pair.) Moses erected the tent, willow mats were spread in the sleeping area and the primus stove, sitting on top of the grub box, was used for the first time. A candle provided light.

There was a strong ground drift as we retired for the night. By early morning, and I mean early, we were covered with a fine dusting of snow which had blown through the flimsy tent. We were both cold. The Inuit, by the way, do feel the cold, but can withstand more than we; they have a higher metabolic rate. This may well have changed now that they no longer spend the winter months in igloos. The cold prompted us to leave without delay. By the light of the moon we were able to prepare for the takeoff. Tough sledging, two more sleeps and much walking finally brought us to George River slumbering under a mantle of snow. The entire trip had taken seven sleeps and we had covered at least 100 miles on foot.

We were very warmly welcomed by Bob May, the post manager. Bob has spent most of his adult life in the north. He and his wife, Nancy, now run a most successful fishing and hunting camp at Pyramid Mountain in the same general area. I had officiated at their wedding, one of my first, and it gives me great pleasure to know that we have re-established contact after a lapse of many years.

The lessons I learned on the journey were to prove invaluable. In the first place, the white fox fur parka was handsome but was quite impractical: the wind pierced it from all directions. Henceforth I would settle for nothing less than caribou skins. The caribou parka (koolituk) was hip length and made from two skins, with the fur outermost: one skin on the front and the other on the back. They were sewn together with sinew under the arms. I have seen a very fancy koolituk with the hides cut into strips lengthwise, white and brown alternating. Such a parka would be most unsuitable for winter travel; regardless of how tightly the skins were sewn together, the interminable winds would blast their way through them.

Secondly, my sealskin boots were impossible. Most Arctic travellers swore by them. I swore at them! My feet were cold from morning to night so I decided to design my own footwear. The HBC manager at Chimo, who had spent a number of years in Indian country, suggested moosehide and kindly ordered skins to arrive on the annual supply ship. A local seamstress drew an outline of my foot on paper and made a pair of moccasinlike boots. The legs, cut from drill, were attached and a decoration of rickrack braid ran from the ankle to the top of the boot, with the customary drawstring. Two pair usually lasted a winter. They were warm and most comfortable. No need to soften them by chewing; just turn them inside out, allow to dry and rub them lightly before putting on again. They were ideal for dry, crunchy snow and had a pleasant aroma. The skins had been smoked by Indians and had the texture of chamois.

Following this trip, I was given my Inuit name, "Pee-jook-tuk" ("The One who Walks"), possibly because I spent so much time either breaking trail or walking alongside the sled.

I later discovered that my guide was able to gauge my speed on snowshoes by walking in my tracks. The length of my stride made it possible for him to calculate my rate of travel.

The Dog Team

Skidoos seem to be the rage in the Arctic these days, but I would plump for the old-fashioned method of transportation any day of the week. Admittedly, this motorized contraption, the "iron dog" as it is called, can cover the ground in a fraction of the time, but would it not take all the fun out of travelling? As I see it, a skidoo has two distinct drawbacks: the first, what happens if the motor dies when one is miles from home or the nearest camp? (The Inuit are very mechanically minded, unbelievably patient, and in some cases might get it going again. I well recall one summer spending several days afloat on a Peterhead boat which had chugged to a halt. The Inuit tinkered with the motor, and as it turned out, had to make a part. With the crudest of tools they succeeded and rather enjoyed the challenge.) Worse still, imagine running out of gasoline miles from nowhere! No such problem with the dog team. If food ran low, we simply struck out for the floe edge, or open water, and claimed a few seal. In most cases one could "live off the land" for a while. If all else failed, one could resort to dog meat. This has been the lot of many an Arctic veteran, but not mine, I am glad to say.

This brings me to my second point: would not the noise of a skidoo careering across the open plain send every living creature in hot pursuit of cover? With their keen eyesight, acute hearing and sense of smell, would they not look for a safe haven at the first inkling of danger? Long-distance travelling can be tedious at the best of times and the sight of wildlife, in all its forms, is one of the pleasures of the trail. The Inuit love to hunt and the prospect of running into a herd of caribou or a wandering polar bear is most appealing. There are no deadlines to be met, so why not make the journey as enjoyable and profitable as possible?

In the language of the far north, the dogsled is always referred to as the "komatik." In earlier times, it was made from whalebone or even walrus hide. The latter was quite adequate as long as the subzero weather continued. It had the added advantage of supplying the dogs with food when late spring arrived and the runners began to thaw. Eventually, wood became the norm. Initially, the Inuit relied on driftwood, but in the course of time the Hudson's Bay Company shipped lumber into the various settlements north of the tree line.

In the eastern Arctic, the average komatik for long-distance travel is 23 feet in length and 18 inches in width. There is a very sound reason for these dimensions. A short sled would bump along the snow and the constant jolting and jarring would soon take its toll on the dogs and impede their progress. An analogy may be helpful. Compare a small craft with an ocean-going liner. In choppy water the boat, bobbing up and down like a cork, would be at the very mercy of the high seas at every turn, whereas the liner would breast the waves and proceed gracefully on its way. In a similar fashion, the long sled spans the ridges and crevices; it glides over the snow bridging the furrows and giving the team a certain rhythm.

Experience has taught the Inuit that wider sleds are not too practical; they sink in soft snow, forcing the dogs to a standstill. In fact, the wider apart the runners the more deeply entrenched they become. This is particularly true in the maowyuk.

A series of holes are drilled in the runners. The wooden crossbars, notched at each corner, are laid on top and extend over the sides. The distance between the crossbars is three to four inches. Sealskin line is threaded through the holes of the runners, passed over the ends of the crossbars, criss-crossed underneath and knotted to hold them in place. So the sled has a certain "give" to it - a certain resilience. It has a fair amount of play, as it were. Nails are never used; in very cold weather they would simply pop out upon striking a boulder or hummock of ice.

Mudding a Sled

The title "Mudding a sled" is a misnomer. Mud, in our sense of the word, is never used. What is used is decayed vegetable matter. It is of the same consistency as peat or turf which is used for fuel and burned in cottages in the west of Ireland. (The thought occurs to me that it might be feasible to extract this substance from the Arctic and produce it on a large scale. The idea might be worth pursuing. Peat is found in Russia, Sweden and Finland and used with varying degrees of success, so why not capitalize on the richness of the Northwest Territory land mass which could prove beneficial to all concerned. Perhaps some young, enterprising agronomist might take up the challenge.)

The mud for shodding the runners is hacked out of the frozen earth. Small clods are dropped into a pot, water is added and the blend put on the primus stove to melt. The resulting mixture has always reminded me of the bran mash given to horses on returning from the hunting field. When melted, the water is drained off and the brew carefully screened for foreign particles. Stones or small hard objects would damage the blade of the jack plane which is used later. The sled is turned over. The steel runners have been removed and replaced with burlap which provides a better sticking surface. With a fistful of mud in each hand, the Inuk commences at the upturned end. The mixture is laid on top of the runner to a depth of about six inches and wrapped over the edge onto the wood which helps to keep it in place. The same procedure is followed all along the runners.

As freezing begins, small, white crystals appear on the surface and it becomes lighter in colour. In fact, by the time the mudding is complete, it will have turned to a pale brown. When solidly frozen, a jack plane is used to round off the runners and make them as smooth as possible. Finally, the Inuk, with a mouthful of water, spurts a stream onto a piece of polar bear fur and runs it quickly over the runners. It takes many squirts to cover both adequately. Such glazing leaves a thin coat of water which freezes instantly. The final product has a glossy appearance and the hitherto light brown has taken on a deeper hue.

The purpose of mudding a sled is to reduce friction - and it does so to a remarkable degree. Place a sled on top of a small hill, set it in motion with the touch of a finger, and it will glide down with the greatest of ease. Even a well-mudded sled, however, needs constant attention. When on the trail, "icing-up" may be necessary two or three times a day. It is a simple task and can be done in a matter of minutes. The sled, with the load lashed on, is overturned. The jack plane takes care of the rough patches, and several jets of water, applied in the usual manner, will suffice until mug-up time again. Patching, if necessary, will take longer and will be of a temporary nature, using caribou moss and water, but it will see one through to igloo time or reaching a campsite.

The Harness

The practicality of the Inuit I found evident in the dog's harness. It is made from heavy duck, or drill, and cut into strips a few inches in width. A loose collar slips over the head. A strip is sewn to the collar at the nape of the neck and runs down the back to the hind quarters. Two more lengths are attached to the collar, one either side of the neck, passing under the forelegs and then securely tied to the central line near the rump. At this same junction, an individual trace connects each dog to the sled. Ivory rings, carved from walrus tusk, are fastened to the extremity of individual traces and the main trace is threaded through them and toggled to prevent slipping. The latter, about ten feet in length, is connected to the upturned section of the runners.

The Dogs

I was always fascinated by the sled dogs. The average team for long-distance travel usually consists of ten to twelve dogs. They are sturdy, compact animals, 50-80 pounds, with powerful shoulders; each is capable of hauling more than its own weight. There is some variation in colour - often a mix of several. Many animals are a deep cream while others are mainly black, or black and white. Puppies are born at any time of the year. During the winter months, the tiny ones may be brought inside the igloo to avoid the bitter extremes of temperature.

The mask, and the eyes particularly, betray what most believe to be their basic origin - the wolf. They certainly share some characteristics; they howl but do not bark, and occasionally wolves and huskies have been seen feeding together.

The leader is the key member of the team; it is usually the strongest, most aggressive and intelligent and will respond readily to commands. It is harnessed with the longest trace which gives it great freedom of movement.

Dogs must be placed to function well together, so the position of each animal is carefully chosen. Strong dogs are found well to the fore, followed by the weaker and less experienced. The eastern Arctic favours the fan hitch, ideal for narrow, bush country conditions where the team may have to travel in single file. Each trace is a different length; dogs do not run side by side, thus fighting is kept to a minimum. The entire team is harnessed many yards in front to minimize the strain and stress of a sled's constant jolting. There are no roads or even trails in the far north; rough ice can be a constant menace, making progress slow and exhausting.

Sled dogs are not bred for pleasure or companionship. Their sole function is work, and hard work at that. A lazy animal can expect the whistle of the lash over its ears as a not-so-gentle reminder that more effort is needed. The Inuit are stern masters, incredibly skilled with the whip, picking out a slacker with ease, but their strict discipline does not involve breaking a dog's spirit. A cowering animal would be a liability, and a good handler knows intuitively how much to demand from each member of his team.

Trading at the Post

Travelling in the Bush Country

On the Trail

Cutting Ice

Kayak

Ptarmigan Lunch

Hunting Party

Two Hunters

A Team at Rest

Building an Igloo

Lighting the Primus

Mudding a Sled

Softening Mukluks

Iceberg

Ice Breakup at Lake Harbour, 1950

Typical Inuit Dress, 1950

Building an Igloo

The real purpose of an igloo is to obtain shelter from the biting blasts of winter's gales. As a matter of fact, when the primus stove and candle have been extinguished, the temperature within is only three or four degrees higher than that outside. When the thermometer dips to thirty or forty below zero, with a wind abroad, survival demands some sort of protection.

Every evening on the trail, at day's end, we must build a shelter. One has read about intrepid souls too tired at camp time to erect a dwelling, who have unrolled a sleeping bag in subzero weather and crawled inside. That would be tempting Providence. In my experience, no seasoned traveller would be so foolish. Were he to do so, he would not survive to tell the story.

Obviously, ice and snow abound in the Arctic, which may give the impression that there should be little difficulty in building an igloo anywhere. However, it is not always possible to find suitable snow. Its consistency is the vital factor. It must come from one snowfall or snowdrift. (The latter, in this case, is a pile of snow heaped up by the wind.) Ice blocks are never used in the construction; they are too heavy and awkward to heave into position and would begin to drip as soon as the primus stove is lighted. Snow blocks, on the other hand, are considerably lighter and the air pockets provide essential insulation.

No tundra inhabitant would ever contemplate leaving home without the required building tools: a snow knife - butcher-like with an elongated blade - and an ordinary hand saw. Both play an integral part in the work at hand.

Using the saw, the builder sticks the tip into the snow and pushes it down until the blade is completely embedded. If it goes down smoothly all the way without interruption, he has struck gold, but if the blade suddenly drops at any point, he knows instinctively that the snow is stratified and the block will split up into layers when removed. In that event, he moves on.

The Inuk's trained eye is a valuable asset in detecting the areas where likely snow may be found, but the depth is another matter and this can be ascertained only by testing. Many a frigid evening I have spent as my guide cast his eyes in all directions hoping for the best. Having found the required substance, he must now make sure that it is in sufficient quantity. The base of an overnight igloo is about eight feet in diameter so, to be on the safe side, he will test the snow within a radius of approximately ten feet. Here it should be mentioned that all blocks will be cut from within the circle. The Inuk will build the igloo around himself. It will not be necessary to go further afield. In this way, one sleeps the depth of a snow block below the outside surface, thus gaining extra protection from the sweeping winds.

Two more preliminaries before our architect is ready to construct the night's shelter. Continuing to use the saw, he removes a block which resembles in shape an inverted pyramid. He cuts at an angle of 45 degrees. Were he to cut perpendicularly on all four sides, it would be impossible to remove the solid mass. This oddly shaped lump is discarded. He is now ready to carve out the first in a series of rectangular blocks which comprise the building material. They measure, roughly, 36 x 24 x 8 inches and weigh anywhere up to 25 pounds. The Inuit are shorter than we, so the depth of a block presents a problem. To overcome this, our Inuk gouges a groove on the face of each block as an aid to extricating it. The blocks are quite brittle and great care must be taken in releasing the base of each from the snow floor. Anything other than a clean cut will herald disaster: a piece can very easily split off. Having carefully dislodged a number, he commences to build.

Two blocks are placed end to end by the edge of the hole and sloping slightly inwards. The topmost edges are mitred so that the blocks will support each other. This principle is followed throughout the entire structure.

On completion of the first layer, or circle, he is now ready to cut the "spiral" to the igloo. Standing in the hole, which will eventually become the floor of the snow house, and using the snow knife, he cuts halfway down one block, then another slice to the right as you face the operation, at an angle of 30 degrees or so. The next block sits rather precariously on top and enables one to see the spiral to good effect. This is the secret to all igloo construction. Without the spiral the walls would get higher, but would never be enclosed. It is now a matter of continuing the procedure until the builder comes to the final block.

The last opening is rather small so one end is pushed through and the block is laid on top. With the snow knife, he slices pieces from all sides of this block until it falls neatly and firmly into place. The last block is the key to the entire construction; without it the shelter would collapse. All the while, our engineer is inside. He has built the igloo around himself. Having cut a small hole in the dome - the igloo must breathe - he removes one of the base blocks and crawls outside.

Meanwhile I have been busy chinking the structure. All the crevices and holes must be filled in with loose snow so that the night's shelter will be secure and free from snow dust. I complete the task by scrambling aloft. Igloos are very solid and can bear my weight with ease. Under favourable conditions, a trail igloo can be erected in about 50 minutes.

Christmas Day in an Igloo on the Open Tundra

"Another pair of hands would be very useful if you plan to reach Payne Bay before Christmas," said my Fort Chimo guide. As money was always a consideration, I normally hired one man and his team. However, on this occasion, I acquiesced, but rather suspected that the purpose of the exercise was to benefit his son rather than me. The boy was in his early teens and his father, Tomasi, understandably was anxious that Lukasi should join us for the experience. As it happened, we were fortunate to have him.

It was not my intention to spend Christmas Day in an igloo, but the vagaries of the white wilderness dictated matters. Several sleeps out of Chimo, we ran into a heavy snowfall and were forced to seek shelter. A snowstorm is one of the few occasions when an Inuk can lose his bearings. All the familiar landmarks are covered and the driving snow makes it impossible to see. It snowed for three days and nights without a break. Before the first day came to a close, we had to turn off the primus stove as our sleeping quarters were getting very damp. The heat from the primus stove and the little heat our bodies generated caused the igloo to drip. Continuous dripping would not only soak our bedding but would also cause problems later on, to which I can well attest from experience. To roll up a wet sleeping bag is asking for trouble, as it quickly becomes frozen. Trying to unroll it results in a tug of war and most of the eiderdown is scattered to the four winds. We ventured out on the fourth day to find that the snow was so deep we began to question our going on. Staying would have meant erecting a new igloo. We left.

December 24th found us a few days from our destination, so we began to build the night's shelter as darkness descended upon us at two o'clock in the afternoon. During the construction, I saw a remarkable phenomenon. The snow began to take on a beautiful pink colour. Gradually this pink colour lifted towards the horizon and moved into the heavens. As it continued to rise, a deep blue took its place and chased it out of the sky. Later the moon appeared with its clear, bright light. An enormous circle encompassed the moon and on its circumference, at points north, south, east and west, were large, radiant blobs. The moon emitted rays like the arms of a windmill, which reached about halfway to the circle. Had they continued, they would have passed through the centre of each blob. This rare occurrence faded all too quickly.

Maintaining body heat is one of the key elements in Arctic travel. While Tomasi was building the igloo, I kept myself warm by chinking it - filling in the crevices to make it as windproof as possible. On this occasion, however, I also bedecked the snow house with dwarf sprigs which helped to capture somewhat the spirit of Christmas. It was so cold grappling the sprays that my hands soon became numb. The work was completed piecemeal. Within the comparative warmth of the igloo, I cut up about fifty, four-inch lengths of Arctic willows and formed them to read, "CHRISTMAS DAY, 1948." These I embedded in the blocks directly above the door. No need to shave on Christmas Day: unheard of on the trail. By this time I had grown a beard. While "Arctic" and "beard" may appear synonymous, such an outgrowth is not really to be recommended, as the reader will later discover.

Our kerosene - paraffin oil - was running low. We had two full travelling days ahead of us so we spent most of the Festive Day without heat. The outside temperature was probably below -20°F. Subtracting four or five degrees from this would bring the inside temperature to about -15°F. A little on the cool side, to say the least. Of course, the primary purpose of an igloo is not for warmth but shelter from the everlasting winds.

I arose at six-thirty and wished Tomasi and Lukasi a happy Christmas. We shook hands. Fully clothed, with parkas on and sleeping bags draped over our shoulders, we prepared for the service of the Holy Eucharist. Taking the chalice out of the travelling case, my fingers froze to the knop. Tomasi, experienced in such matters, removed them, skin intact. I carried a small bottle of wine each day on the trail and took it to bed with me every night. Warm water from the kettle was added to it before pouring into the chalice. The top of the grub box served as an altar, with a candle either side and a small cross in the middle. With the exception of a corporal - the cloth on which the paten and chalice are placed - linens were non-existent. My ecclesiastical vesture: a stole, which was all that I could manage.

The service began. In our branch of the Catholic Church, the celebrant - officiating priest - receives the sacrament first and then administers to the congregation. Realizing that my fingers and lips might freeze to the vessels, I did not raise them to my lips, but received by intinction - dipped the wafer into the wine. I soon discovered that a thin film of ice had formed on the surface so had to pierce it with my finger. (The Roman Catholic practice would have simplified matters considerably: wafers only.) I administered the wafers to Tomasi and Lukasi respectively, who followed my example. We attempted to sing a few Christmas carols but were not too successful. At the conclusion of the service, I had to pour hot water into the chalice to thaw the ice crystals.

One never knows what to expect on the trail so it is always advisable to be prepared for any emergency. I had brought a few luxuries should the worst happen. Our Christmas dinner consisted of noodle soup, canned spiced beef and dehydrated potatoes which tasted like cardboard. I well remember the name of the company which concocted this mush, but will refrain from mentioning it. To this day, I avoid their products. A tin of peaches, and coffee with powdered milk completed the menu. It was not particularly reminiscent of Christmas, but a welcome change from regular trail fare.

No sooner had we left our Christmas quarters than we ran into another team which was returning to Payne Bay. Jonasi had been visiting his traplines. The proof was on his sled: six white foxes. As two dog teams always work better than one, we were delighted to see him. Besides, Jonasi had several lake trout on board which he gladly shared.

Our last night on the trail together was memorable. As it is not always easy to find suitable snow for building an igloo, we travelled for more than two hours without success. At one stage, Tomasi and our new-found friend were contemplating putting the two sleds together at right angles to each other, and spending the night open to the elements. The idea did not greatly appeal to me. I persuaded them to continue the search. Finally, in a vain effort to reach land, the sleds became embedded in the rough shore ice. Disgusted, the Inuit left the sleds suspended and the dogs spread-eagled over the ice, and crossed on foot. Within half an hour, they had reached the far side and found suitable snow to build a house.

It was decided to unhitch the teams and abandon the sleds overnight. We proceeded to unlash them and carry the bare necessities to land. Darkness had long since fallen. We stumbled and fell over the enormous hummocks, 20 feet in height in places. I can still see Tomasi falling over one and dropping the grub box. It crashed below, totally shattered, and our precious supplies descended to the depths. We retrieved what we could, but the grub box was beyond recall and we consigned it to an icy grave.

Goods and dogs safely ashore, I went for a walk while the igloo was being built, and promptly became lost. It was an eerie sensation finding oneself in the vast white wilderness and not knowing where to turn. The intense silence and stillness of the land were overwhelming. I tried to retrace my steps, but had lost all sense of direction. (At the best of times I have a poor bump of locality.) I climbed one hillock after another. At length, I came to my senses and decided to take a stab at one more hill. If that failed, I could sit there until the search party arrived. When lost, one is always advised to stand one's ground and conserve as much energy as possible. From the top of the hill I could see the shore ice and the igloo - a blessed sight. Igloos are translucent and can be seen from a great distance. There was no need to say that I had been lost; it was perfectly obvious. I was a reasonably hardened traveller by this time so they were not unduly concerned.

The moon made its appearance as we were having supper at nine-thirty. Despite the late hour, Tomasi and Jonasi decided to collect the remainder of our paraphernalia. We unlashed the sleds and hoisted them, one at a time, onto our shoulders and carefully made our way to the shore, slipping and falling all the while. The sleds did not escape unscathed; hunks of mud had broken off and had to be replaced before the final day's journey. Decayed vegetable matter, the "mud," was very plentiful and it did not take long to hack it out of the ground. The preparation of same for a runner was another matter. The work was completed by two in the morning and we crawled into our sleeping bags.

The following morning, the sleds had to be planed and iced-up before lashing on the load. The guides, resourceful as always, mounted the steering wheel on top of the sleeping bags. A ground drift was swelling as we pulled out. A few dogs were cruising along and not pulling their weight. With deadly accuracy, the long whip lash cracked over their ears. This gentle reminder was all that was necessary. The going was excellent and we sailed along over lake and tundra. The inevitable mug-up, that hallowed hour, came about midday. A semicircular snow wall was assembled to shield the primus stove. These stoves are quite temperamental and it is very difficult to get them started in windy weather. The lighted methyl hydrate in the cup flickers and goes out with the slightest breeze.

In the late afternoon, we could see the settlement of Payne Bay. It looked quite close. But close is a relative word. Distances across snow can be very deceptive. In this case, it turned out to be about 20 miles. Still far from our journey's end, the dogs began sniffing the air and giving tongue. Like foxhounds or gun dogs, they rely upon scent rather than sight. When eventually we struck the beginning of a well-beaten trail leading directly to our destination, the dogs, sensing the end was in view, put on a final spurt and we rolled in at eight-thirty. The Payne Bay dogs, alerted, were howling their heads off as we arrived. In a flash, the few tent doors were thrown open and greetings exchanged. Unfortunately most families had departed; they could not afford to wait for my arrival. So much for our Christmas excursion to the western shores of Ungava Bay.

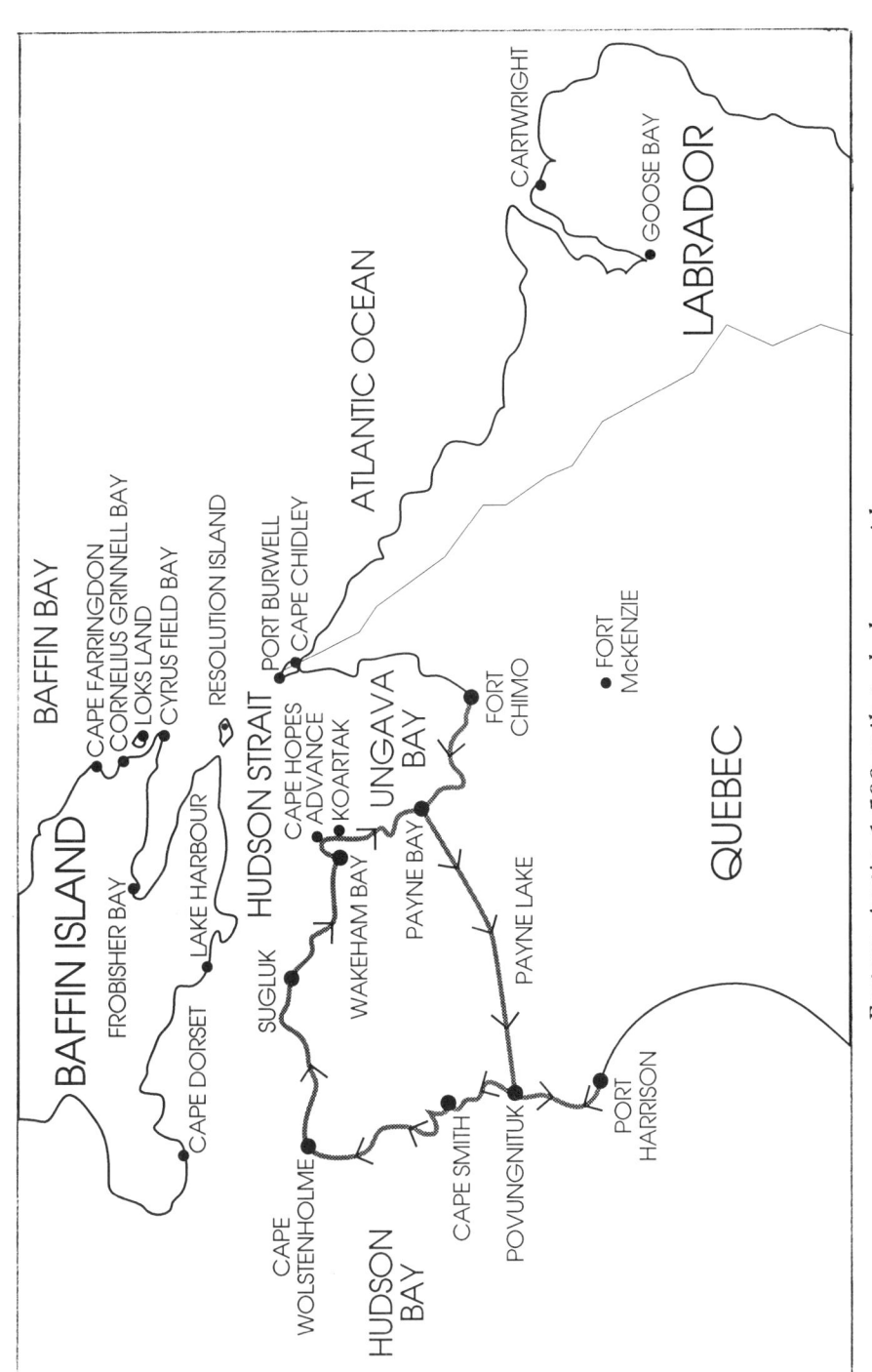

Eastern Arctic. 1,500-mile trek shown with arrows.

Fifteen Hundred Miles by Dog Team: A Winter's Journey

My diary of February 14th, 1949 reads, in part:

> I departed from Fort Chimo this morning and am bound for Port Harrison, a settlement on the eastern shores of the Hudson Bay. I am hoping to go cross country, setting out from Payne Bay and, if successful, reaching Povungnituk on the Hudson Bay, a few sleeps from Port Harrison. I shall be the second white man to have made the trip during the winter months.
>
> The crossing of the Ungava Peninsula was effected by a white trader many years ago, but he almost lost his life and nobody has attempted the journey since that time. It is reported that he reached Povungnituk by himself and in a state of exhaustion; his two companions had perished on the way. According to his story, they had died from starvation. When the trader recovered, there was a trial; it was thought that he had turned cannibal. Quite naturally nothing could be proved.
>
> In view of the foregoing, I have been strongly advised not to attempt the crossing. However, I am willing to take the risk and the natives are agreeable. The arrangements have been completed by Tom Crawford, Post Manager at Payne Bay, and Wulfert Tolboom, Post Manager at Povungnituk. Tom will furnish me with all details upon my arrival at Payne Bay.

I shall always be indebted to Tom Crawford and Wulfert Tolboom for the time and effort spent on my behalf; without their willing assistance and co-operation this trip could never have materialised.

Upon reflection, the story of my crossing seems rather far-fetched. Having read my account, readers will be in a better position to judge for themselves. One thing I wasn't quite prepared for: the intense cold in the interior. I was accustomed to -50°F, but hadn't bargained for a frigid -70°F. In those days one did not include the wind-chill factor.

With two winters' travelling experience behind me, planning food for the trail was down to a fine art. Gone were the canned goods. Instead, I made an Irish stew of sorts. It was easy to prepare. More to the point, it could be reheated in a matter of minutes and with the least amount of effort.

A large pot was set on the stove, and cans emptied into it: vegetables and a variety of meats. There was no difference in taste and the labels were little guide as to contents. One often wondered how long the animals had been dead before canning! Pork and beans, sausages, a few boxes of spaghetti, macaroni and dehydrated potatoes were added as well. This mixture was brought to the boil, allowed to simmer for a while before being scooped into greased trays, and transferred to the warehouse to freeze. When it reached the consistency of fudge, each tray was scored, and when well frozen the slabs were broken into pieces. These, in turn, were dumped into pillowcases and left in the warehouse until needed. Tea biscuit was still a favourite and the ever-popular hardtack biscuits.

Arriving at Payne Bay, I was fully briefed. The post manager and the Inuit guides had insisted that teams should leave Povungnituk and Payne Bay simultaneously, and meet at Payne Lake, which was about the halfway mark. There were very good reasons for this decision. The idea of two teams setting out from Payne Bay en route to Povungnituk was out of the question. The amount of dog food alone required for such an undertaking, would have been in the neighbourhood of 1,700 pounds. Besides, 500 miles would have been a long haul, regardless of the condition of the huskies. Weather and travelling conditions had also to be taken into account. All in all, it was a wise decision. I was the guest of the Crawfords for a few days before launching out.

The day of our departure must have been a rare sight. The residents stood nearby to wish us well and to cheer on the six teams. The teams, each one vying for the lead, fairly tore up the trail out of the settlement. We set our initial course southwest until striking a river running east and west which eventually brought us to a small lake. After a noontide mug-up, the five accompanying teams fanned out in all directions to visit their traplines. They rejoined us later in the day and we all spent the night at a local camp.

The families in the camp were living in tents rather than igloos. This is unusual in the barren lands. The occupants rushed out to welcome us. No sooner had I asked Matthew, my guide, where I should spend the night than an elderly woman grabbed me by the arm and said, "Khi-git," which means "Come." I was escorted into her tent and treated like royalty. I was the celebrity on this occasion, but she would have afforded the same kindness to any visitor. She helped me to take off my caribou parka (koolituk), windproof trousers and boots. She threw the latter to her daughter, Nancy, and instructed her what to do. Nancy had probably never seen my kind of boot. I had long since abandoned the traditional mukluks in favour of moosehide footwear with canvas tops. Nancy turned them inside out, rubbed the soles together and hung them up to dry.

The "Matriarch" provided me with a cushion, a flour bag filled with eiderdown, and placed it on the edge of a bunk in front of the small stove in which willows were burning. While we were chatting, she saw some foreign objects on the bunk and proceeded, talking a blue streak, to brush them off with a ptarmigan's wing. It was a most comfortable tent. The floor was covered with willow mats. These Arctic shrubs also burn very well, but the stove requires constant attention. Not only do they throw a wonderful heat, but they also give off a most pleasant aroma reminiscent of a gypsy campfire by a country lane.

One of the problems of tent dwelling in the winter months is the shower of crystals which float down when the stove is allowed to go out at bedtime. Fine snow particles form under the roof as the tent gets colder and spray everything in sight. Many a night I slept with my tuque on to keep my head warm and dry.

The following day was typical of these parts: the wind blew, the snow drifted and it was very cold. However, it did not really affect us; we had decided to remain as the sled needed attention. It also gave me the opportunity of visiting the families and taking a double wedding. To be able to take a wedding "on the spot" so to speak, may appear unusual, but one has to consider circumstances which prevail in the north. The idea of calling banns, or obtaining a licence, is quite foreign to our Inuit people. And their nomadic way of life makes pre-marriage courses difficult, to say the least. A frank talk during the ceremony is about all that is possible.

In the course of my ministry I have encountered many an emotional bride, but this Inuit ceremony was quite an eye-opener. As soon as the first hymn commenced, one of the brides began to sniffle, then the other. Soon they were sobbing convulsively. The relatives joined in, and before long the tent was reverberating with deep, heartrending wails. One might well accept such a display at a funeral, but that was never the case. The Inuit philosophy of life includes the belief that tragedy is of a piece with one's existence. If a violent death occurs, they are stoically accepting.

When the service proper began, all was quiet. At the conclusion, we had another hymn - the Inuit love to sing - with the same watery result. Singing seemed to strike an unfortunate chord!

It was at this camp that we picked up our Inuk guide, Paulasi. He was an elderly man, relatively speaking, and one of the few in the district who had been inland as far as Payne Lake. Paulasi invited Mark, another veteran, to join us for the trip. Six teams pulled out from the camp. The day was clear but cold, and the westerly wind swept over the treeless wastes. Our sled lead the way. The accompanying teams lagged behind tending their traplines. Soon they were out of sight. About midmorning - camp had been struck at six o'clock - as monotony was setting in, my guide decided to go fishing. Paulasi, familiar with the topography of the terrain, crossed the rough shore ice and headed south to a lake. Here we tried our luck jigging. Paulasi and Mark, bending down, brushed the surface snow aside and peered in. They were trying to find out the thickness of the ice, and came to the conclusion that it was about three feet. That's a lot of hacking. They took turns. The fragments of ice were removed with a scoop. One lake trout, about eight pounds, was the only catch, but it was more than sufficient for our evening meal. We retraced our steps, striking the Payne River again.

As we moved along, Paulasi pointed out a number of traps which had been set close to the riverbank. When we came upon a live fox which had been caught, we halted and put the unfortunate animal out of its misery. I must confess that my initial reaction to this method of ensnaring wildlife was one of repugnance. Approaching the victim, one could hear the sound of clinking metal. The animal's eyes were bulging out with fear, and its heart was thumping away like a runaway engine. The lead foreleg had been locked in the steel jaws of the trap. To avoid being bitten, Paulasi distracted the fox by touching its nose with a stick. Its sharp, gleaming teeth made their mark. Meanwhile, Paulasi grabbed the tail, extended the animal and firmly placed the sole of his mukluk on the heart. Death was almost instantaneous.

Continuing our journey, we called a halt in the early evening and began to build. We were safely ensconced in our snow house when the other teams began to trickle in. Two igloos were sufficient to accommodate the hunters. And what a harvest! One beaver and twenty foxes in all had been trapped. There was one pale blue among the number.

Paulasi and Mark rose at five o'clock. All was dark. The moon had disappeared. When on the trail, the Inuit always light the primus stove immediately. They simply roll over in bed and kneel on the caribou skin mattress with the eiderdown quilt draped over their shoulders. Methyl hydrate is poured into the cup and set alight. When sufficiently warm, the stove is pumped to get it going. It is now time to dress and have breakfast: the usual simple fare of tea and hardtack biscuit.

Clearing the igloo of its contents, I scrambled into my koolituk and prepared to leave. But first I shook hands with our fellow travellers; they had reached the westerly limit of their traplines and were heading home by a circuitous route. Their parting words: "Good sledding and good luck." We were certainly going to need it.

Feeling somewhat deserted, I began to walk and left Paulasi and Mark to lash the sled and to harness and hitch up the dogs. A clear crisp day greeted us. The cold westerly wind was still abroad, and with the temperature somewhere in the high -40°sF, I had to maintain a brisk pace. Heading into the wind, getting colder by the minute, I trudged along the river, my cheeks and nose feeling the brunt of the blast. I could sense frostbite and had to spend much of the time thawing out the various parts. The process is simple but costly: remove a mitt and place the hand on the affected area until life is restored. Replace the mitt to warm the hand and begin all over again. It is a vicious circle. To add to the discomfort, I was sporting a beard. Icicles literally hung from my moustache, and the tip of my nose suffered in consequence. The mound of ice was a daily companion and could not be removed until evening when I hung over the primus stove until the offending mass had dripped away

My early morning saunter over, we set off with the sled. The going was very tedious; the snow lay deep all along the river and the runners of the sled were scarcely visible. It was time for a mug-up and a rest. The dogs were feeling the strain and the runners needed attention. Since leaving Payne Bay, we had covered about 75 miles. With another

425 ahead of us, I began to wonder if we would ever make it. Feeling a little gloomy too, perhaps, Paulasi and Mark pulled up the team in the late afternoon with a view to building the night's shelter when we could find suitable snow. We skirted the shoreline but the snow was stratified. We carried on upriver, testing as we went. Almost two hours had elapsed before we were successful. This was our third night on the trail.

The next morning, during my constitutional, I noticed something dark on the landscape. Thinking it was a rock pushing its head out of the snow, I paid little attention to it. Later I discovered it was a snowy owl. When within 50 yards or so, it took off upriver and pitched further on. As I advanced, it followed the same pattern. The fourth flight was its undoing; it landed on a mound and walked into a trap. As I approached, it fluttered and hissed and made frantic efforts to free itself. I awaited the team. As Paulasi bent down, the owl thrust its sharp talons into his parka, releasing its grasp only as the guide killed it. In keeping with the country, life and death are harsh in the Arctic. I saved the skin and eventually had it mounted. Paulasi and Mark had boiled owl for supper. I preferred the Irish stew.

Continuing the struggle, we spent the afternoon battling the elements. It was bitterly cold, and the temperature dropped perceptibly as we journeyed inland. Winter had begun to tighten its grip

From time to time, temperatures have been mentioned. These of course are only approximate, but not entirely guesswork. Coal oil is the yardstick by which temperatures can be estimated: -50°F is its freezing point.

By nightfall, the temperature was in the mid -50°sF. The coal oil was frozen in the primus stove. My hands were so numb that I could hardly strike a match, much less get the primus stove going. I held a lighted candle under the primus until the solid mass began to run. This, incidentally, became a routine chore until we reached Hudson Bay. I started the procedure as soon as the igloo builders began construction. We hauled the coal oil can inside the snow house each night to keep it warm.

Another bleak day lay ahead of us. It was not an inviting prospect. The wind was still a factor, and I began to weary of the omnipresent ground drift. Visibility was fair, but Paulasi insisted that I should not attempt to break trail but rather stay with the team. As we drove headlong into the snow drift, our faces received the full blast. My cheeks and nose got the brunt of it, and Paulasi's cheeks were also showing signs of frostbite. Both men were feeling the pinch, but stoically pushed on. Thankfully. a few more hours along the way, Paulasi called a halt and tested the snow with a view to building in for the night. Again we had snow problems. As it turned out, the blocks used were decidedly on the thin side and only delicate handling enabled Paulasi to complete the work. Under normal conditions, the blocks would be considerably thicker and there would be no danger of a cave-in. Mark built me a small snow wall to shield the primus stove. I could never have managed without it.

We were safely inside, or so we thought, and having our evening meal when we heard a great disturbance outside. The dogs, which are usually quite content to curl up and relax at day's end, became restless and three jumped up on the igloo. Pushing open a snow block, Mark dived outside and scrambled on top. A few blocks gave way and he came crashing through. He sent the kettle of water flying, soaking our mitts, duffel socks and sleeping bags, which had been laid out for the night. Paulasi had been cooking a bannock over the primus stove. The heel of Mark's mukluk landed on it and broke one of the arms of the primus stove supporting the frying pan. Meanwhile, we were being showered from on high: the swirling snow descended in the form of a white blanket. I volunteered to clean up the mess while Paulasi and Mark attempted to unearth the tent and cover the gaping void.

Drying our clothes and bedding took some time. The sleeping bags were still damp when we crawled in. All was peace and quiet. But not for long! One of the guy ropes securing the canvas gave way and a corner of the tent was flapping for all it was worth. This, I felt, was the last straw but Mark, imperturbable as always, jumped out of the sack, put on a minimum of clothing, grabbed a snow knife and departed. He called to Paulasi and explained what he had in mind: cutting a hole in the snow wall and passing the rope inside. It was wrapped around the grub box and firmly tied. Mark plugged the hole and returned. A cold, miserable night ensued. When morning rolled around we were too cold and tired to move on, and decided to spend the day resting and drying our gear. We built another snow house and were more than thankful to vacate the old one.

We had been travelling the river for days and now changed course. Crossing the rough shore ice to land without mishap, we continued to veer west. The ground drift had subsided, travelling conditions had improved, but the extreme cold was a continuous headache. Paulasi pointed me in the general direction and I sallied forth onto the open plain. The team picked me up shortly. The rest had obviously benefited the dogs as well. We could sit on the sled without unduly taxing them. When the going got a little sticky, Paulasi "paddled" with his left leg to give us an extra push. Freezing of nose and cheeks persisted, but there was little that could be done about it. It was a case of "grin and bear it." We took advantage of the favourable conditions, and carried on until early evening before digging in for the night.

As the sled was being lashed, Paulasi greeted me with the words: "Providing all goes well, we should arrive at Payne Lake sometime today." This was joyful news indeed. Even the dogs seemed to sense that something was astir. Casting around like a pack of foxhounds, they were anxious to get a move on. The sun had barely made a nodding acquaintance when we beheld a glorious sight: a windbreak - the semicircular snow wall used to protect the primus stove when making a brew. Like Daniel Defoe's Robinson Crusoe, "we were not alone in this desolate land." It was the first sign of human life in this central region. Travelling into the void for days on end at the mercy of the elements is an odd experience to say the least. It is indefinable. Words cannot convey the intensity of the feeling.

Return to the windbreak. Here, the POV (Povungnituk) Inuit had left a note to the effect that we would meet them, not as previously arranged at the highest point of ground on the southern shoreline, but about half a day's journey further on. Their igloo, the note went on, was built beside a small hill. It all seemed rather vague to me, but Paulasi said that he would have little difficulty locating it. Somewhat disappointed, we carried on and at mug-up time cached some of the dog food for the return journey. It eased the dog's burden and gave them a bit of a break.

In the early afternoon as the sun's rays grew dimmer, Paulasi spotted someone on the lake and drew our attention to him. My guides were wild with excitement and exclaimed in their Inuit tongue, "Inuk, tekoeet?" ("Do you see the Inuk?") Out of character they danced and jumped into the air and shouted, "Nakomik. Nakomik." ("Thank you. Thank you.") They pushed the dogs for all they were worth. In the midst of all the excitement, Paulasi, poker-faced, casually remarked, "It is only a rock!" Drawing closer, we could see the POV Inuk standing on the lake. He was brandishing a snow knife and seemed just as delighted as we. With a sealskin bag slung over his shoulder, a rifle in one hand and his knife in the other, he hobbled along. The dogs slid to a standstill. We jumped off the sled and hugged the beaming stranger, Willie. We said how thrilled we were to see him and he made a fitting reply. Willie leaped on the sled and guided us to his igloo. We were a few days behind schedule, but the POV Inuit were not too concerned; time has little meaning in the north.

Willie and his friend Jacobi had been off hunting in the interior and had bagged four caribou and landed two-dozen fine lake trout, the largest measuring almost four feet. Needless to say, we had caribou steak for dinner. It compared very favourably with filet mignon but hadn't the same staying power. In true Inuit fashion, my Payne Bay guides were given choice cuts of caribou meat for their long journey home. We loaded some on board too, and cached the rest in the igloo for safekeeping. A number of traps were set around the snow house to discourage predators. The day we arrived at POV, two sleds were dispatched to pick up the booty.

And so came the parting of the ways. I thanked Paulasi and Mark for their thoughtfulness, and still marvel at their resourcefulness. It had not been an easy trip. But little did we realize what lay ahead of us.

On a day fit for neither man nor beast to be abroad, my new guides and I drove into another snow drift and biting cold - a taste of things to come. In short order, the ground drift blossomed into a full-blown snow drift. We were heading into God knows where, and the visibility was rapidly approaching zero. All too quickly we were engulfed, and the force of the wind on the dreary, rolling plain was unbelievable. It swirled around us and struck from every angle. Our caribou parkas were coated in snow. Ice needles lashed our faces. My nose became a "bloody mess" and felt as if it had been slashed with a scalpel. I made the great mistake of draping a handkerchief over it, only to discover that it froze to the blood. It stopped the bleeding, but removing it was another matter.

Sitting amidships, I could see neither Willie nor Jacobi. They, in turn, couldn't see the tips of the runners, much less the dogs. I got off the sled to run alongside to keep warm and found that was a feat in itself. Fearing that I might be swept away at any moment, Willie tied a strip of sealskin line to my wrist and strapped the other end around his waist. He tugged it periodically to make sure that I hadn't lost touch. On each occasion, I responded to set his mind at ease. We pursued our course relentlessly. Such was our lot for several days. So the question arises: "How did Willie find his way?" Impossible? Read on.

I assure the reader that guesswork did not enter into it. One does not wander without purpose in this inhospitable land. Willie was not perturbed in the least; he had a sure-fire method of determining the route. Let me explain his system.

Every Inuk knows the direction of the prevailing wind. It alone will permanently mark the snow. Suppose, for the sake of argument, the prevailing wind is coming from the north. Its force will produce arrowheads - all pointing north. Assuming in our case it was due north, Willie simply struck the arrowheads at right angles; we were travelling due west. When the blistering drift had finally lost its force, we were right on course.

To find these arrowhead markings, which lie below the surface, it would be necessary for me to go down on bended knee, sweep aside the loose snow on top and see for myself. Not so Willie. With the ball of his foot, using a circular motion, he could "feel" them. Noticeably as we proceeded, he would paw the snow from time to time. If there was any doubt, he would halt the team and make a more thorough investigation.

An early night was on the agenda. Despite the storm, Willie built the igloo in record time. The dogs were fed, and immediately curled up looking like white balls in the frosted snow, tails covering noses to facilitate breathing.

The wind must have roared all night, but we were oblivious to it. As the floor of an igloo is the depth of a snow block below the surface, we were well insulated. In any event, the drift was still in high gear as we set forth. And what a foul day! We changed course and sought the comparative shelter of the river. Reaching the centre was a challenge. The mounds of shore ice were formidable. Weariness had set in and we gave up the struggle. Rather than haul the sled and its contents over the piles of ice, we set the dogs free and carted a minimum of supplies to shore. Tea, bannock and raw frozen lake trout sufficed for our supper.

Long before daybreak, we retrieved the sled and our gear. The komatik needed attention; chunks of mud had been gouged out. We spent the day, thank heavens, repairing the runners and the dog's traces. The latter, due to the criss-crossing of the dogs and the sharp edges of the ice, were showing signs of wear. Willie, not too adept with needle and sinew, re-enforced them with sealskin line. Only in cases of emergency will a man actually condescend to sew anything.

If yesterday had been a foul day, today was absolutely unbelievable. We were forced to abandon the struggle about high noon. Unequal to the task, two of the dogs, as if on cue, dropped in their traces and lay prostrate, gasping for breath. Willie, knowing instantly what was wrong, pulled up the team and went forward. Their lungs simply could not function under such adverse conditions. The Inuit are very much in tune with their animals; their welfare is of paramount importance. They depend upon one another; they are, in fact, a unit.

We were now faced with the coldest part of the trip, although good food and a good day's rest had worked wonders. Once again we changed course and drove headlong into the drift. We jogged for the greater part of the day to ease the dogs' burden. Mercifully, the wind gradually died down and a light ground drift followed. We took advantage of the improved conditions, traversed the uplands and spent the night beneath the shadow of the hills. The unremitting cold remained a constant irritant.

We entered one of a number of passes and continued to climb zigzag for several hours. Riding on the sled was out of the question. Walking, heaving and pushing were much more to the point. Reaching the summit, we had a panoramic view of the surrounding countryside. The air was clear, crisp and biting and the visibility, for the first time since leaving Payne Bay, was superb. What a vista! Looking west, we could see the Hudson Bay - our destination. So near and yet so far. Five days, not to be without misadventure, lay before us.

It was too dark and treacherous, and the dogs too fatigued, to carry on. In a hollow there was an abundance of suitable snow. Willie and Jacobi began to build in for the night.

As dawn broke, we were on our way again. Barrelling down the hillside was great fun, but decidedly dangerous. It took expert handling on the part of Willie and Jacobi to land us safely and intact at the end of a run. How they avoided the rocks and boulders as we flitted past, I shall never know. Wind whistling through the network of passes had packed the snow and made travelling conditions excellent. Taking every precaution necessary, we used the brakes throughout the descent. The brakes are circular bands or hoops of sealskin line, one thrown over the tip of each runner. I had been given my instructions by Willie before we attempted to go down: "Sit as close to me as possible; the extra weight will make the brakes more effective." When we arrived at the bottom, the next assault began. We spent the day winding our way through the maze of passes. At least it gave some respite from the everlasting winds.

Snow drifts have been mentioned on numerous occasions throughout the journey. The reader may be at a loss to know exactly what is a snow drift. It has often been identified with a whiteout, but there is a considerable difference between them. According to one authority, "a whiteout is a condition in which the sky, the horizon and the ground become a solid mass of dazzling, reflected light, obliterating all shadows and distinctions." A snow drift, on the other hand, is a condition in which the loose snow on the surface is blown up into the air by the force of the wind, reducing visibility to zero. Rather similar, one imagines, to a sandstorm in the desert.

A new day dawned, and with it more excitement. Still among the hills, we struck a river and followed its course to the lake below. Brakes in place, we started the descent. More than halfway down, the guides suddenly leaped off, heaved the sled to one side and jammed it against a rock. Seeing the cataract, I jumped to safety. Willie and Jacobi, ever on the lookout for danger, had avoided a flight over the falls and a possible early demise. The dogs were unhitched and the sled eased to the brink. I would estimate the falls to be about 50 feet in height during the summer. Now frozen over and the bottom filled in with snow, the drop was probably 30 feet (and not too gradual at that). Jacobi tied the thong of the whip to the rear of the komatik and with Willie at the helm, the sled was set in motion. With 700-800 pounds on board, they were unable to maintain contact for long. As the speed increased, Willie jumped clear and Jacobi released his grip. The sled rushed headlong, overturned near the bottom and came to rest without any damage. Jacobi shooed the dogs down and they were rehitched. As a safety measure, they left the sled still on its side. One couldn't be too careful. Willie untied the line, coiled it and threw it up. Jacobi lowered me down. For his part, he wrapped it around the boulder and when he ran out of line, slid the rest of the way, making sure to hold onto one end

On our way again, we reached the lake and stopped for a mug-up. Four more days, and a continuous snow drift, brought us to Povungnituk.

I shall never forget the morning I first saw the Hudson's Bay Company buildings. That vision, for vision it truly seemed, is as vivid today as it was half a century ago. For over three weeks our whereabouts had been a matter of conjecture. We were somewhere in the vast stillness of the white wilderness. Now the silence had been broken.

I have at least an inkling of what Peary must have felt when the Pole was within his grasp. Treacherous days, appalling travelling conditions and bone-shattering cold lay behind, and a sense of achievement must have pervaded the party. Peary and his companions had gone out into the unknown and survived to tell the story. How much easier it is for present-day adventurers. It is one thing to set out with the sure knowledge that if the task proves impossible and death stares one in the face, a plane can be on hand in a matter of hours. It is quite another matter to venture forth knowing full well that death might prove to be more than a possibility, and that this fact was inescapable. I am not trying to downgrade the North Pole enthusiasts of our time. What I am trying to say, and I do not think it an unfair comment, is simply this: there was no backup for the Arctic explorers of the nineteenth and early twentieth centuries; no emotional security in the form of aircraft hovering overhead to bolster their spirits and ensure a safe return. Such groups were at the mercy of the elements, and had to be resigned to risking all in a bid to decorate the Pole with the flag of their country.

Missionaries, even in the forties and fifties, had no means of contacting a friendly aircraft. We had no radios when travelling. If one got into difficulties, one extricated oneself or perished in the attempt. Life was hazardous, but excitement and exhilaration fired the energies of youth. These are memories never to be forgotten.

The moment we reached POV, the post manager, Wulfert Tolboom, sent a message by Morse code to Port Harrison to say that we had landed, a little battered but safe and sound. We were not a very presentable lot. Our cheeks had suffered frostbite and my nose was still split from the intense cold. Perhaps the wound would heal in milder weather, but it continued to bleed from time to time. It was never a very handsome appendage, but frigid temperatures hadn't improved matters.

Here, at POV, I met Wulf and Wanda Tolboom again. Our first meeting had been a brief encounter on the RMS *Nascopie* in the summer of 1946. In common with all the HBC Factors and their wives, they showed me the greatest kindness and consideration. And Wulf had gone out of his way to oversee all the arrangements for the second leg of the journey to POV. I was at last able to thank him in person.

Two sleeps and a fresh team brought me to my ultimate destination, Port Harrison. Temperatures had eased considerably and the dogs, sensing journey's end, galloped along. We travelled several miles out to sea. The sea ice is the highway of the north and we took full advantage of it. Its long, unbroken stretches can be monotonous, but with our destination assured we gave the dogs their head. It was the easiest and most pleasant part of the trip.

Port Harrison was a veritable city compared with Fort Chimo. There were six white households: HBC, Department of Transport, RCMP, Nursing Station, an independent trader and the Anglican Mission. I stayed at the mission house; the resident missionary was on furlough.

I had a glorious three weeks and was entertained lavishly by the populace. I scarcely had a meal at the house. In fact, I was having such a wonderful time that the chilling thought of another seven or eight weeks on the road - the coastal route was 1,000 miles - was having a dulling effect on my enthusiasm for travel, but I had to reach Fort Chimo before breakup. It was now April and time became an important factor. At least March, the most unpredictable month of the year, could now be forgotten, but by Arctic standards, April is still very much winter. Better weather wouldn't brighten our path for some weeks. However, once the decision had been made, I soon got into the swing of things and the thought of lengthening days was encouraging.

The snow buntings, heralds of spring, were already making their appearance. The males were the first to arrive, followed a few weeks later by their mates. The migration lasted about six weeks - a joyful reminder of warmer times ahead.

The coastline is punctuated with settlements, and I visited each in turn. Apart from "parish" visiting, it was necessary to replenish the food supply and hire another team to take me to the next village. The distance between the settlements varies greatly: some, a few sleeps; others, anything up to five or six, all depending upon weather and travelling conditions.

Time was of the essence so we pressed on. En route to Cape Wolstenholme, situated on the most northerly point of land overlooking islands in the Hudson Strait and the Foxe Channel, we made two stops for refuelling and change of teams: one at POV and the other at Cape Smith.

We travelled throughout on the sea ice. The going was excellent, but tiresomely uniform. We could see Cape Smith jutting out into the bay days before reaching it. As the crow flies it is about 200 miles from Port Harrison, but the days seemed endless. The sun glistened on our pathway, but it continued bitterly cold. The Hudson Bay is the coldest body of water in the entire Arctic. As Peter C. Newman in *Company of Adventurers* reminds us, "Few places on earth experience such extreme weather fluctuations. Because it is out of reach of moderating ocean currents, Hudson Bay is more frigid than the iceberg-packed Arctic Ocean or the North Pole itself. Temperatures of -80°F have been recorded - colder than most polar lows."

Each evening we crossed mounds of shore ice before setting foot on land to build the night's shelter. At first reading, this might appear a simple matter, but be not deceived. Many an evening, hours would elapse before reaching the safety of the shoreline.

The approach to Cape Wolstenholme is quite spectacular. We took a corkscrew course up the side of a mountain and reached a high point within several hours. The descent, with brakes working overtime, was equally zigzag. At length we entered a narrow gorge with towering mountains and cantered into the settlement.

Wolstenholme stands in a most commanding position, but no one was there to greet us. It now lay derelict. The HBC buildings were still standing, but the Company had abandoned the post. We decided to build an igloo rather than spend the night in the deserted dwelling house.

A brief stop at Sugluk and we were on our way to Wakeham Bay. We took the cross-country route. As we approached a lake - the country is teeming with them - we ran across an Inuk who was about to remove a net from the icy depths. The net had been set in the early winter when the ice was merely a foot in depth. It may be of interest to know exactly how a net is set under the ice. With a long-handled ice chisel, John had hacked a hole in the ice about one foot in diameter. When water was struck, an immediate jet gushed forth. The broken chunks were removed from the hole with a scoop. To prevent the hole from freezing over, handfuls of snow were dumped in. Even in the coldest temperatures, this will keep holes open for several hours. In the middle of winter, lake water will make ice at the rate of a quarter inch per hour.

A series of holes was chopped out. The distance between the holes is about five feet, and the number of holes depends upon the length of the net. This particular net was 20 feet in length, so five holes were necessary. The net was now laid out on the snow with the cork floaters, spaced at intervals, on the top and lead weights on the bottom. An eight-foot pole was placed alongside one end of the net and a corner of the weighted section was attached to the bottom of the pole. The top was similarly secured to the pole. A long sealskin line was fastened to the other extremity of the net to prevent it from floating free. The pole, with net securely in place, was threaded through the first hole and pushed down into the water. When floating, two poles were used to guide it to the next hole. This procedure was followed until reaching the final hole.

John now grabbed the tip of the floating pole, pulled it out of the water, leaving the butt end (with the net attached) submerged. The pole was raised aloft and stood perpendicular in the hole. Meanwhile chunks of ice were thrown in to keep it erect. John now went to the first hole, pulled on the line and dragged the end of the net out of the water. It was fastened in like manner to the lower portion of the pole and raised on high. The rope was neatly coiled and buried, together with pick and scoop, in a mound of broken ice and snow. The protruding poles marked the spot.

To remove the net was a simple matter. One pole was hacked free. The net was removed and a line attached to it. Failure to do this would cause the net to float at will. It would eventually have to be reset - an almost impossible task in high winter. While pulling the net onto the ice, John said to me, "There are some fish." He asked me to take the net in my hands and "feel" them. All I could feel were my hands getting colder. However, he assured me that there were a few, and continued to haul the net out of the water, piling it carefully at his feet and removing each fish as it came to hand. The catch amounted to five nice lake trout. He very kindly gave us two.

The net was reset. One end was attached to the pole and inserted in the water. John now went to the other extremity, pulled on the line and the net was dragged through the hole, re-attached to the pole and set in position. It was as simple as that!

Continuing our southeasterly course, we came upon a second large lake. By the shore we saw another dog team. To my naked eye it looked more like a rock than anything else. However, I accepted Toonoo's word. As usual, he was right. Our new-found friend awaited our arrival so that we could make the crossing together, but within an hour we had lost touch.

As we eased our way onto the lake, the sun was splitting the heavens, which we hoped augured well for a safe crossing. It was glare ice, flecked with islands of hard-packed snow. These proved to be our salvation. Soon the wind arose, and in short order we were being driven at intervals by relentless gusts - so much so that Toonoo was seriously thinking of retracing our steps to the safety of the land. But the month of May was now upon us and I was a long way from home, so prevailed upon him to carry on. I was soon to regret this decision.

For two hours we battled the gale's might. Completely at the mercy of the wind, we were driven hither and thither, all the while perilously close to open water. It was rather terrifying. On the lead side of the sled, facing a watery grave, we tried to haul the team towards land. A vicious blast forced us to lie along the sled, dragging our feet on the ice in an effort to guide it to safety. It was all in vain. The dogs, stumbling and falling over one another, were powerless. They were unable to gain a footing and were eventually dragged along the ice by sheer momentum of the sled. Presently the sled slammed into a hummock and we were forced to abandon ship. It catapulted into the air and came crashing down broadside and eventually slithered to rest by a mound. Appalled, we watched our precious cargo take a pounding. Toonoo and I lay on the ice until the rage subsided somewhat. Between gusts, we crawled our way to the sled. Toonoo said it was much too risky to stand; another burst might blow us to oblivion!

Reaching the sled, we were horrified to discover that one of the dogs had been killed. At some stage the sled must have run over it. Characteristically, Toonoo showed little emotion; he removed the harness, lashing it to the sled, which remarkably had survived. Missing chunks of mud from the runners seemed to have been the extent of the damage.

The worst had passed, but a few more anxious moments lay ahead. Finally, and with a sigh of relief, we pulled in to a safe haven and began to patch the runners. And patch is the operative word, caribou moss and snow being the only material available. It sufficed to get us to our destination. Miraculously, the other team escaped unscathed. We had lost sight of each other before the mishap but eventually joined up before nightfall.

I shall not easily forget my first visit to the Roman Catholic mission station at Wakeham Bay on the Hudson Strait. Father Schneider, the priest-in-charge, and Brother Cheral greeted us on arrival. Formalities concluded, I said to Father Schneider, "Where shall I stay?" meaning, of course, which igloo? Without hesitation he said, "With us, of course."

Whereupon he instructed the brother to collect my belongings. Meanwhile Father Schneider showed me into the guest room and told me to make myself at home. He retired to the kitchen, returned with a jug of hot water, handed me a towel and said, "The brother will prepare you a meal while you are having a wash-up."

At one time, the Government Radio Station was housed here at Wakeham Bay, but had moved to Cape Hope's Advance on the northwest tip of Ungava Bay. The buildings had been acquired by the Roman Catholic Church.

It was a large house, with two chapels no less, and a number of spare rooms. Very graciously, Father Schneider placed one chapel at my disposal. A charming host of the old school, he had been born and brought up in Belgium and was a Priest of the Oblate Order of Mary Immaculate. He spoke several languages fluently, among them English and Inuktitut. He was also a talented artist. He showed me some magnificent water colours which depicted various scenes in the life of the Inuit people. His masterpiece, which I was able to see only in a photograph, was hanging at that time, the lay brother whispered, in Milan Cathedral. Father Schneider was delightfully reticent and I had to pry much of the information out of him. The brother was a keen photographer and did his own developing and printing.

On my second day at the mission, Father Schneider said to me, "For dinner this evening we are going to have the delicacy of the north: whale brain." I was almost ill on the spot! It resembled large earthworms. I had eaten, as I imagined, every conceivable Arctic dish, but this, my host assured me, was the *pièce de résistance*. He may well have been right. In any event, a few glasses of excellent mass wine before the meal had a miraculous effect. Unfortunately, the result of the wine was beginning to wear off when we sat down to table. I plunged the fork into the spaghetti-like heap. As I continued to struggle, Brother Cheral, without comment, rose and returned with a bottle of wine and proceeded to replenish my glass. The exotic dish was becoming more palatable by the minute. The balance of the meal slithered down without undue discomfort.

The time had come to say farewell to my hosts. Brother Cheral had filled our grub box to overflowing with appetizing delights. I couldn't thank them sufficiently for their great kindness and expressed the hope that they might visit me in Fort Chimo. Unfortunately, it never came to pass; Roman Catholic Missionaries were not encouraged to travel beyond parish boundaries and Chimo lay far to the south

A fresh team, thanks to my new friends, was standing by as I made final preparations to continue my journey. One has to accommodate oneself to changing climatic conditions, particularly with regard to clothing. The koolituk (caribou parka) had been discarded in favour of the duffel parka with the usual windproof cover. The parka hood was trimmed with wolverine - the only fur which will not freeze in subzero weather.

Drill overpants had taken the place of caribou trousers. Reluctantly, I had to forego my moosehide footwear. The boots were a godsend in the bitter weeks crossing the peninsula, but not designed for wet snow. Early mornings in spring there is a frozen crust on the top layer, but as the day wears on the snow begins to lose its crispness, even becoming slushy at times, and the waterproof qualities of the mukluks are essential. Sunglasses were indispensable. Jimmy, my new guide, had a pair of homemade goggles carved from driftwood, with a slit for the eyes and blackened on the inside to cut the glare.

Jimmy made some adjustments to the team necessary for spring travel. Mud was removed from the runners and the dogs were shod with booties to protect their pads from the needle-sharp granules of snow. They also prevented snow balls from getting between the toes and causing lameness.

A final wave of the hand and we were off. A day's trekking across the bay was slow and tedious. It was late in the evening when we struck the shore ice and immediately met stiff opposition. The winter's deposits of jagged ice boulders were formidable and fading light didn't help matters. (Ungava, unlike northern Baffin Island, does not experience twenty-four-hour daylight in spring.) For several hours we heaved, stumbled and fell countless times. (This may appear an exaggeration, but not so. I can vividly recall a trip when I travelled for two days over ice ridges, and at day's end could look back and see the igloo in which we had spent the previous night. This was on Frobisher Bay which has the second largest rise and fall of the tide in the world.)

As we chopped and wove our way through the endless mass, the main trace snapped and the dogs took off. The gathering gloom swallowed them up leaving us to ponder our next move. Jimmy went in pursuit and eventually tracked them down. Ironically, the ice held them fast. On his reappearance we decided to camp. Jimmy unloaded the necessities and pitched tent when we finally scrambled to smooth ice. Spitefully he refused to feed the dogs. Despite the fact that it was May, we spent a cold and uncomfortable night. In the early morning we could feel the movement of the ice. The tide was coming in and massive chunks were heaving and groaning nearby. Jimmy's comment was brief: "Let's move - and fast!" We did, but it took the best part of an hour to emerge.

The dogs' traces were wearing thin; the constant rubbing against the razor-sharp edges of the ice had played havoc with them. Nevertheless, we forged ahead until reaching Payne Bay, the post from which I had set out for the eastern shores of the Hudson Bay in late February. I spent a most enlightening evening listening to Jimmy regaling his hearers with my exploits! I had no idea that my present travelling companion was a noted raconteur.

The Inuit love to talk and gossip - but without malice. After all, what else is there to do during the long winter evenings. For several hours, Jimmy gave a graphic description of my journeyings since leaving Payne Bay many sleeps ago. He had them hanging on every word. Guffaws, "E"s and "O"s accompanied many a story. I couldn't understand everything that was said, but got the general drift. Judging by the faces of his audience, and the shy glances thrown in my direction from time to time, nothing was lost in the telling.

What was the source of his information? The bush telegraph had been at work. I had spent several days at most settlements and encampments to rest up, replenish my food supply and hire fresh teams. During these brief stopovers, my guide would give an account of my trip to date, highlighting the more notable aspects. Multiply these tales many times and that will give some idea of the garbled versions rendered by Jimmy. Is it any wonder that they were spellbound?

Now I was on the last leg of my pilgrimage. John, a Payne Bay Inuk, was my guide and we were bound for Fort Chimo.

The coastline is wrinkled with bays and inlets. John was a little concerned about breakup and, as if reading my mind, suggested that we make straight for Chimo. I was all in favour.

The tide was on the ebb, so discretion and extra care were necessary. Normally, supplies are distributed fairly evenly along the sled, but the perils of spring travel during the breakup of sea ice made adjustments essential. We were about to spend many dangerous hours bounding over the ice pans, and if we were to make it at all, the dogs' movements must be as unrestricted as possible. To facilitate matters, most of the weight was now shifted, concentrating it at the front of the sled. Too heavy a load at the rear could easily drag sled and team backwards following an unsure leap over open water.

In the first bay, the movement of boulders and floating ice cakes was clearly visible. It was a simple matter to skip from one large pan to the next, but the comparatively small "rolling" boulders proved to be a very different situation. John had to give the dogs full rein so that they could jump without restriction. Frequently, some would fall short of the mark and plunge into the frigid water.

Meanwhile the others, spread-eagled over several floating hunks - ten dogs couldn't get a footing on one - waited impatiently until we had retrieved the lost and dragged the sled to the brink. Here, we gave them enough rope to make the next leap. When the yawning crevasse was too wide, we pulled the sled to the verge and threw the dogs over, one at a time. The long komatik bridged the gulf with ease. Imagine trying to control such a seemingly unruly team and maintain course. John had unlimited patience and the ingenuity of his kind. On a large pan of ice, a rest and mug-up were a welcome interlude. The blistering sun bore down upon us as we untangled the traces and prepared tea. Snow crystals, which form on top of the ice pans, were scraped into the kettle. It was mildly brackish. Large hardtack biscuits, dunked, and clear tea revived us.

John knew there was a camp in the vicinity so he headed the dogs in that direction. A few more hours of hopping, skipping and jumping and we crossed to land. The igloo was deserted - and leaking. (May is a little late for igloo dwelling.) Nonetheless, we unloaded our gear and made ourselves at home. As we were brewing tea, Pootagook, his wife, Sarah, and two teenagers arrived overburdened with ptarmigan. After a reasonable interval, we decided to try our luck.

At this time of the year the birds are putting on their summer plumage. The neck of the willow ptarmigan is the first part to change. The feathers are dark brown, tipped with scarlet. There is a streak of scarlet over each eye. The tip of the tail is black. We shot fifteen between us, usually a fair bag for an hour's work, but actually not many considering the number abroad. They were running and cackling all over the place. It was very easy to track them down. Telltale imprints on the melting snow among the willows were their undoing. Sarah prepared supper. Ptarmigan are never plucked. They are skinned, feathers and all, and dropped into a large pot suspended above the blubber lamp. I opted for fried game, little realizing that the cook would use rancid seal oil. I chose two plump birds and suggested white meat only. Actually, the breasts are a dull grey and not nearly so gamey as those of their grouse cousins. Our hosts and John did justice to the meal. Each bite, liberally coated with congealed seal oil, was avidly consumed. It was all "finger-lickin' good."

By the time we vacated the dripping igloo, the sun had long since arisen. Its searing rays blistered my lips and my nose resembled a glowing beacon. We had to contend not only with direct sunlight, but also the ultraviolet reflected from the snow. The Inuk's sallow, oily skin apparently afforded him considerable protection. If he experienced any discomfort, he certainly didn't show it. For my part, I was forced to cover my nose and lips with a handkerchief, folded diagonally and tied at the nape of the neck, bandit style. It was a frightful nuisance, but helped to cut the penetrating rays. Even after almost fifty years, my lips are still incredibly sensitive.

We continued to leapfrog over the floating mass. Realizing that our destination was just on the horizon, we took so many chances that something was bound to happen sooner or later and we would suffer the consequences. We came to grief a few hundred yards from shore. John, rushing forward in an attempt to pull out two floundering huskies, slipped and landed in the salty foam. I tried to pull him out. Instead, I joined him! The month of May notwithstanding, it was icy cold. John grabbed the main trace and managed to scramble onto the ice. I followed suit. With the trace and John's assistance, I was able to extricate myself. We peeled off our clothing, including underwear, and stood briefly stark naked. After a brisk rubdown and a change of clothing, we were off once more. With the help of the incoming tide, we reached shore and pursued a land course parallel to the Kuujjuaq River. Presently, Fort Chimo came into view. What a sight! To avoid further mishaps, John waited until we were directly across from the settlement before venturing onto the river. It was still solidly frozen. We must have crossed the mile and a half in record time.

The residents, Morris, Bernice and Jerry Wright, the RCMP, George Mackay, and a handful of Inuit were on hand to welcome us. I was invited to spend the night at the HBC post. George Mackay joined us for dinner. I was bombarded with questions and we literally burned the midnight oil.

It took me several weeks to get back on track. I was bone weary, and the lack of vitamins on the trail had had a telling effect. It was some time before my system returned to normal. To look at us, we were the colour of polished copper. One might have suspected that we had spent the winter in Florida!

A postscript. My annual report, in due time, was dispatched to the bishop. It included an enthusiastic account of my visits to the Inuit and a few delightful days with Father Schneider. What a frosty response! I was berated for "fraternizing" - the episcopal word - with a Roman Catholic priest! "I would build an igloo," the letter went on, "outside the door of his house, rather than accept his hospitality. On no account are you to stay at an RC mission again." I could not believe my eyes. As the bishop had spent about twenty years in the field, one would have thought he might have tumbled to the unwritten code of the north: "A travelling white man, regardless of race or creed, automatically stays with another white man." The Inuit have long accepted the practice and think it perfectly understandable. If the situation were reversed, they would follow a similar pattern.

I have stayed with the Inuit in their igloos on countless occasions and greatly enjoyed their friendliness and generosity. It was not a case of choosing the comfort of a mission house over more austere living arrangements, rather it was the acceptance of an established custom. I was presented with an ethical problem. Clergy swear canonical obedience to their bishop and when I was ordained in Ireland such vows were taken very seriously. After much reflection, I decided that here was a case of situation ethics: the greater good must outweigh such a narrow and short-sighted injunction. If I continued to be at odds with the bishop on this point, I felt that at least God would understand.

Today, many religious attitudes have changed for the better in an effort to reflect more properly the Christian ethic. We are all quite ecumenically-minded and a rather tolerant atmosphere among various denominations prevails.

Fort Chimo to Lake Harbour

Under the auspices of an Irish Missionary Society, I had entered the Arctic in August 1946, on the understanding that I would be expected to do a three-year stint. As mail was very infrequent, only three or four times a year at most, I wrote to the bishop two summers later requesting details about my return to civilization in the summer of 1949. The letter was posted on the annual supply ship. I received, in due course, a somewhat curt wireless message from him informing me that all missionaries were required to do a five-year term and that I was no exception to the general rule. (In my day the HBC managers knew Morse code and were able to transmit and receive messages by wireless.) As I was sponsored by the Missionary Society and simply "on loan" to the Diocese of the Arctic, I really was under no obligation to the diocese and very politely made my point.

However, I had always wanted to see the barren lands, and now an opportunity presented itself. I made a deal with "Archibald the Arctic" and sent the following communication: "Will be prepared to do two more years provided that arrangements can be made for me to proceed to Baffin Island next summer." Realizing that there was no alternative, he capitulated. And so it was in the summer of 1949, I left Fort Chimo for my new home, Lake Harbour, travelling by boat.

Max Dunbar had been staying with me that July and perhaps as a thank-you for my hospitality, had offered to take me at least part of the way, as he would be continuing his work along the coastal waters. His boat, the *Calanus*, lay at anchor in the Kuujjuaq River opposite the HBC wharf. We had a farewell dinner with the Wrights, and Bernice spent much of the evening trying to persuade me not to move. We had formed a very congenial trio - Morris was always available with help and advice and I had spent many happy evenings as their guest. While I made other friends in the Arctic, they still stand out in my memory.

Bernice produced coffee and sandwiches about eleven and then Max went off to check on the boat, leaving me to say goodbye. How I hated these last farewells. As a parting gift I had planned to give the Wrights an electric coffee pot - something Bernice had wanted for a long time. The HBC boasted electricity and the present would have been helpful with so many guests. An officer from the air base had offered to bring me one from the U.S. on his last trip - but he had forgotten all about it. Somehow or other I had managed to get hold of some cash and while I would have preferred the pot itself, I gave them an envelope with money and an explanatory note. Undoubtedly they would have better luck with the purchase than I. As we were leaving for the dock, Morris caught my suitcase in the screen door. The case flew open and the contents were scattered on the ground. The ensuing search for lost articles eased the tension and we all had a good laugh.

A dinghy took me out to the *Calanus*. Accommodations were a bit tight as there were nine of us on board. I slept in Max's cabin (the laboratory). We left the next morning on the full tide, but at the mouth of the river heavy fog enshrouded us and the Inuit pilot suggested a return to Chimo. The Wrights were in the middle of lunch, but somehow did not seem too surprised to see me. Bernice felt it was an omen and that the whole trip was doomed!

Two days later we were off again in beautiful weather heading for the George River, where we anchored the next day. Bob May met us with his canoe and invited us all to lunch at the post. The mosquitoes and sand flies were abroad by the million. Ignoring their attentions, I went for a long walk, camera in hand. The rest of the party were having a preliminary celebration; Bob and Nancy's new baby girl was to be baptised that evening. Before the night was over some of the guests were in an expansive mood, to say the least. Bob cleared the floor for dancing, dumping the living-room rug outside the front door. The engineer, who had sprained his ankle a few days earlier, rolled himself up in it and tried to go asleep. Max volunteered to teach us some Scottish reels, including the Sword Dance. One of the others, whom I am hesitant to identify, also performed. One couldn't say he danced, but he certainly did reel.

The next stop was Port Burwell where Max intended to spend most of the week. Noah Anatok arrived after breakfast and I decided to accept his brother Henry's invitation to stay with them. Later in the afternoon Henry and I walked to a sheltered harbour three or four miles to the rear of the settlement. While my host was cruising the cove in his skin boat looking for seal, he came upon a shark he had shot a few days previously. It was the first I had ever seen. What an ugly brute!

The local Inuit were planning a number of sealing expeditions and invited me to join them. On one trip we travelled in a scow with two kayaks and two skin boats on board. As we neared the open sea a killer whale was spotted, but no attempt was made to hunt it. The Inuit are wary of these whales. We continued to hug the shore cruising the islands, occasionally having some luck. Rain had begun to fall so a tent was pitched on the deck to shelter us.

The seal hunt continued for several days as we threaded our way among the islands. We were able to anchor in a tiny harbour where the water was very deep and it was possible to bring the scow close to the rocks. The Inuit were anxious to gather some driftwood - a precious commodity not easily found in this treeless area. Henry and I broke off sealing hoping for a polar bear, but all we found were old tracks. We climbed a small mountain and then traversed rocky ground and stony valleys. From the top of the second peak we had a most beautiful view. It would have made a wonderful photograph, but unfortunately I had run out of film. It was not unlike Connemara, or even the rugged Kerry coast. I could well imagine how cold and austere it might look in the winter.

Returning to the scow we discovered the rest of the party had been more fortunate; the day's bag numbered twenty seal. Setting our course for Burwell we ran into poor weather and high winds. The scow was too old to battle rough seas and heavy waves so we changed direction slightly, running much closer to a chain of islands. The wind eased and the passage to Burwell was not so difficult. As we entered the harbour, we passed Max and his assistants jigging for cod from the dinghy. They would mark each fish they caught and then toss it back. At the dock the seal were distributed among all the hunters, the owner of the scow accepting a larger share.

The first week of August had slipped away and the weather was changing. Snow fell one morning and continued into the afternoon. Henry's family helped me to collect my belongings for my return to the *Calanus*. Max said If the weather improved, Resolution Island would be our next stop. In spite of heavy fog, the navigator suggested that we might make the Button Islands which were not too far. It would save an hour the next day. The waters seemed calm as we left port, but gradually the wind rose and the seas grew mountainous. We rolled heavily with deck awash and water gushing through the scuppers.

Without exaggeration, some waves topped the wheelhouse. A mist was falling but we managed to find a narrow neck between two islands and paused briefly, thinking we might shelter here. Simon, the pilot, was not satisfied and preferred to look for a more secure anchorage. We eventually found an excellent harbour.

Simon's sense of alarm was well founded - a gale howled for the next three days. I began to wonder if I would ever reach Lake Harbour. Max made a sudden decision: he said that we must return to Chimo to drop off Bill, the engineer with the sprained ankle, who was due back at McGill within a fortnight. Max himself needed extra fishing gear which he planned to collect at the same time. Still promising transportation for me, he suggested a more direct route for our return - Chimo to Cape Hope's Advance, then on to Wakeham Bay and finally to Lake Harbour.

However, leaving the Button Islands, we saw an American ship passing through the Grey Strait perhaps bound for Chimo. Radio contact was made and the captain agreed to accept Bill as a passenger. Max had to do without his extra gear but said that he could manage, so we changed direction once more and headed for Cape Hope's Advance.

I was the only one to go ashore. It was interesting to see the settlement in the summer; my previous visit had been during the winter of 1947. The new officer in charge was Fred, a former acquaintance. He lent me a razor and I had a proper bath thinking that I ought to spruce up a bit. Lake Harbour was almost on the horizon - or so it seemed at that moment. After dinner, my host gave me a large bag of cookies, some marmalade and a loaf of fresh bread to take back to the *Calanus* berthed at Koartak, well within walking distance.

Mid-August approached with more dense fog rolling in. The weather was obviously changing and winter not that far off. At seven o'clock one morning, Max roused me with a bit of a bombshell: he had decided to cancel the next leg of the trip and return to Chimo after all. There still remained ten days' work for him at Payne Bay before his return to Montreal the first week in September. Time was growing short; so many days had been lost because of bad weather and he could not risk further delay.

Feeling so close to my ultimate destination, I tried, over the air from the Cape, to arrange an alternate passage. The government ship, *N. B. McLean*, was in the vicinity and the captain agreed to call for me on his way to Resolution Island. An entire day was spent trying to raise the post manager at Lake Harbour to see if the RCMP boat might be going to Resolution and could pick me up there to complete my journey. It was impossible to get through and fearing that I might be stranded at the Cape, I returned to Chimo rather unwillingly, feeling a bit of a fool.

It was to be ten days before I could make another attempt at what now seemed the impossible. The Wrights insisted that I stay with them although their faces sometimes wore an "I told you so" expression. As always, they couldn't have been kinder.

Still en route to Lake Harbour

Thursday, August 25th, and a third attempt to leave Fort Chimo. That week I had contacted Stan Bailey, the Family Allowance Administrator for the Northwest Territories whom I knew quite well. He was then at Port Harrison with a government plane, making an inspection tour of Arctic posts. A spare seat in the plane could have solved my problem. Again I was unlucky; the plane had returned to civilization for repairs, its schedule delayed by three weeks. A stopover at Chimo seemed unlikely that season. An Inuit boat to Payne Bay was my last resort. There I could await an Inuit Peterhead boat travelling to Sugluk the third week in September on its way to Lake Harbour. I had lots of time to make the necessary connections, even allowing for poor weather.

The Chimo boat was quite small and normally used for whaling. It was rather open, except for seven or eight feet sparsely covered in at the bow where I was expected to sleep. In spite of its size, it was very fast. The first night at anchor was not a success. I awoke very early to find that my sleeping bag was soaking wet; the hatch had been left open and the rain was pouring in. Fortunately my cases had been covered with the sail. We skirted the shore all day and sighted a pod of whales about eight in all. They seemed to be heading for a little cove and although we were well within range, we tried to get in closer. This proved to be a great mistake, and we lost them. Rain continued, accompanied by a fierce gale all night long. My "pillow," consisting of my parka, shirt and pullover, was saturated and my sleeping bag quite beyond description. In addition, I was lying in a pool fed by water running down inside the boat. When the sun came out before lunch we stretched all the sleeping bags on rocks by the shore and managed to get them partially dry. We had a brief stroll on land and picked and ate cranberries and blueberries. The sea was finally calm and we reached Payne Bay the next day.

I went ashore by kayak; our boat had been moored well out. Many Inuit came to the wharf to shake hands. I was told that the Sugluk boat had arrived and was waiting for me. We left very early next morning on the full tide. After five minutes running, the engine died. It was not a good sign. The men spent three hours tinkering with it and finally got it started again. At the mouth of the river we were bucking a strong wind and heavy seas. Progress was very slow and we kept close to the shoreline. We halted several times and visited Inuit camps whenever possible.

On August 31st we pulled into Cape Hope's Advance using the sail for added power. The waves were high, continuously lashing the shore which was dotted with rocks. The little boat had a perilous crossing and was often in danger of capsizing. Finally on land, I collected my mail and walked over to Koartak where I was staying with Father Steinman and Father Le Chat at the mission.

Fifty miles to Wakeham Bay lay ahead of us and another early start was in prospect. We refilled our water barrel in a sheltered place. The wind was starting to blow harder and the men wondered if we should continue. Everyone was anxious to get on so it was agreed that we should make an attempt. We were forced to head due north out of the bay to meet the colossal rollers head on. To go diagonally, our shortest route, would have spelled disaster. When sufficiently far out, we turned west and the raging sea swept us along. Our skipper certainly knew how to handle a Peterhead in rough water and there was little cause for alarm. He was normally an amusing companion, but for several hours he neither spoke nor smiled.

Bad weather dogged us repeatedly for several days and we began to have further trouble with the engine. Wakeham lay at the far side of a promontory which could be seen in the distance, and we headed directly for that point. The sails were hoisted but the breeze was gentle and the motor sputtering. The latter failed completely 12 miles from the settlement. Two more hours found us at the mouth of the bay without a breath of wind. The men continued to work on the engine all evening and into the early hours. Having neither their patience nor mechanical ability, I went to bed about midnight.

The following morning found us in exactly the same place as the night before - both geographically and mechanically! The Inuit were cheerful and confident that they could get the motor to go. A kayak arrived carrying a two-gallon can of gasoline - a thoughtful gift from Father Schneider who hoped that this might be our problem. Amazingly, a slight breeze began to ruffle the waters and as it increased, the sails filled and we started to move. Eventually, anchor was dropped and we rowed ashore. Wakeham's setting was spectacular in summer. High mountains flanking the mission were blanketed with a deep carpet of rich green moss. The sandy beach was lined with tents pitched just above the high-water mark.

As I reached the mission house, Father Schneider, who was not expecting me (he did not know I had been on the boat), was tending his wind charger. I called to him and we greeted each other warmly. I so enjoyed renewing an old friendship. Two pleasant days at Wakeham and the engine was finally in running order. The best part of two day's travel brought us to Sugluk.

I now had a fortnight to fill in before the arrival of the *Rupertsland*. On one of my many excursions visiting the tents, I came upon hundreds of geese. The birds were migrating to warmer climates in the U.S. They would return here in the spring, then fly farther north for nesting. They would rest at various stages en route and Sugluk was one of them. That night there was a heavy fall of snow. My hosts during this period were the long-suffering Swaffields. I felt guilty imposing upon them for such an extended time but really there was no alternative. In keeping with all the Hudson's Bay managers I had met, they were hospitable and generous.

At long last, the *Rupertsland* steamed into the bay and I was able to join her for the final part of my journey. With stops and starts, and many unexpected difficulties, my travels had taken two months! The arrival of a ship was always notable in every settlement and Lake Harbour was no exception. As we neared the dock I could see the families from miles around who had gathered on the shore to greet the new residents, a teacher and a nurse. Hope for me had long been abandoned and my late arrival entailed endless explanations.

New Beginnings

Lake Harbour, on the southwest coast of Baffin Island, is one of the most picturesque settlements in the eastern Arctic. I can speak with some knowledge of these parts; I have visited all the coastal communities from Cape Dorset to Arctic Bay on Admiralty Inlet hard by Lancaster Sound.

In the late 1940s and early '50s, Lake Harbour was a tiny hamlet by any standard. There were two Inuit families and four white households: the HBC, the nursing residence, the Anglican Mission and, over the hill - quite literally - a detachment of the RCMP. Why the mounted police authorities had decided to build the station across the harbour is best known to them. At certain times of the year, notably spring and fall, they were completely marooned. No doubt some bright spark from "the outside" had made the decision.

My new rectory was larger and better equipped than the Fort Chimo house. Its chief joy was an indoor convenience, a bit prehistoric (the Arctic term was "honey bucket") but situation took precedence over style. I was now living in the tundra, far beyond the limits of the tree line, and so was dependent upon coal to heat my quarters. The expense was staggering. Coal, delivered by the supply ship, cost $100 per ton and I usually needed fifteen tons for the year. My annual salary had jumped from $1,200 to $1,500 at the time of my move, so it seemed as if fuel alone would overdraw my account. However, the diocese paid the freight which meant that I had a few dollars left over for food and other necessities. All travelling expenses were taken care of by the diocese as well. Guides were paid $2 per day and their families fed at church expense during their absence.

The church building had been constructed by the Inuit from lumber shipped in to the settlement. The church was larger than my previous one and served a wider area. Frobisher and Cape Dorset were part of my parish, but neither had a church building. I still enjoyed travelling and looked forward to meeting more of my congregation at these two points.

Scarcely had I settled in at my new post than the RCMP invited me to join them on a walrus hunt. Needless to say, I jumped at the offer. We were not going out simply for sport or ivory tusks. The main purpose of the trip was to provide dog food for the winter. The police in the Northwest Territories were very well equipped for work in the Arctic. They kept a fine team of dogs for winter travel and the motor launch, for cruising, was quite splendid.

Two and a half days' travelling brought us to an Inuit camp at Frobisher Bay. A day at the camp gave me the opportunity of holding services with the Inuit and visiting their families. The following day we set our course for Loks Land - the most southerly island on the eastern shores of Frobisher Bay. The actual bay is about 130 miles in length. It has the second largest rise and fall of tide in the world and its waters can be very treacherous at times. Day two found us at anchor in one of the many inlets, within easy reach of the island. We were now close to the hunting grounds. More blustery days forced us to remain in the safety of a cove. When we awakened on the third, the wind had died down considerably, so we moved on.

In the vicinity of Loks Land, there was no game at all. Rather than circumnavigate the small island, we turned due north. Leaving our safe little haven, we proceeded through the Lupton Channel - a most impressive waterway flanked by high, snow-clad mountains. A driving, bitterly cold wind and flurries heralded the fast approach of winter. Rounding the most southerly point of the Baccy Peninsula, we entered the swollen waters of Caress Field Bay. We hugged the shoreline briefly and reaching a point directly opposite Farringdon Cape, crossed the bay. The wind had now ceased and the bay presented no problems.

Continuing north, we had our first glimpse of walrus. There were about eight in the herd. I was quite intrigued watching them splashing and weaving in the water. Walrus, so cumbersome on land, were agile and almost streamlined under water. When within range, the junior RCMP and I fired. The Inuit, realizing that this was our first walrus hunt, very courteously refrained. As soon as the first shots rang out, the herd dived, but their slow unwieldy forms on the surface water provided easy targets. (It takes time for a 2000- to 3000-pound walrus to turn over.) A few shots, at least, found their mark. All on board, eager now for the fray, joined in the sport. We closed in on our prey, shooting five in all.

Walrus and seal are well padded with blubber during the winter months, but shed much of it in the summer, with the result that they will sink in short order. Time therefore is a major factor. We were able to retrieve only three; two had sunk to the depths before we could spear them. Harpoons, already assembled on the deck, were thrown into action. A steel rod protrudes from a long, wooden handle. The barb, with a sealskin line attached to it, is mounted on the pointed tip of the rod and held in place by stretching the line along the handle. One fires the harpoon, javelin-wise, and the barb penetrates the tough hide and remains embedded. The handle falls off, floats on the water and can be picked up later. To maintain contact with the walrus, an inflated sealskin is tied to the line. These buoys not only hold the mammals fast, but also indicate their location.

We proceeded to pick up the kill. As we drew near, snorting and honking greeted us. The roaring was quite deafening as the beasts lunged out of the water charging the floats as they came down. Soon we put them out of their misery. Paulasi slit the snout of each, passed a sealskin line through it, and tied the animals to the boat. The water was too choppy to haul them on board so we were forced to seek the shelter of a secluded cove.

We raised them out of the water, one at a time, with pulleys: one attached to the mast and the other about three-quarters of the way along the boom which had been hoisted. This, insofar as the police and I were concerned, was the only hard work of an otherwise perfect sporting event. Paulasi, an old hand with the butcher knife, was ably assisted by Jonasi. It was a time-consuming job. The carcasses were cut up into five segments. By the time the operation was completed, it was too late to put out to sea again.

The following morning was sunny and calm and excellent sport was anticipated. Taking advantage of the good weather, we were on our way by six in the morning. Cruising along the northern shore of William Island, we spotted three walrus. We harpooned one but they all escaped us for a space. We caught sight of them again and soon were dragging all three into the safety of Cornell Grinnell Bay. En route, we saw a herd of ten. Of these, we accounted for five, but due to scarcity of floats - we had only four inflated sealskins on board so had to resort to an empty ten-gallon drum to maintain contact with the fifth - we were forced to allow the balance to escape.

Continuing the chase in the afternoon, we struck out across the bay and fell upon another small herd - six in all. We shot five, but only succeeded in getting four aboard. One large bull sank before being harpooned. This was, without question, the most successful and enjoyable day's hunting. Towards evening, we were kept at anchor by wind and hail which swept the bay.

Another day dawned. Anchor was weighed at six o'clock, but as we reached open sea the water was far from calm. There was an appreciable swell and large rollers struck us from all angles. Eventually, we were compelled to seek shelter in a long, narrow inlet. On our way in we saw three walrus, shot and harpooned them. We continued down the waterway and dismembered them. Due to more unfavourable weather, we dropped anchor for the night.

We awoke to a beautiful morning: cold and sunny but calm, although Cyrus Field Bay was still very choppy. Notwithstanding, Paulasi decided to leave. Heavy seas made a rough crossing. By the time we reached Lupton Channel, there was a gale abroad. To prevent the boat from taking water, for we were heavily laden, we took a zigzag course. The wind funnelled down the narrow passage. In open water again, the waves were throwing white caps. Riding in the teeth of them was far from pleasant and Paulasi decided to drop anchor in a nearby cove until the storm abated.

All was peaceful the next morning. Should we continue the hunt or return home? Reason prevailed. We had achieved our purpose of restocking the dog food for the coming winter, and decided to let it go at that. We set sail for the Inuit settlement at Frobisher Bay. Darkness had fallen by the time we arrived. The sky, for the most part, was overcast, but the light from the west, reflecting on the now calm water, guided our path. In the distance we could see a ship, ablaze with lights, at anchor. It was the government's annual supply ship - the *C. D. Howe*. After a ten-day hunt we were far from presentable: unshaven, unkempt, our parkas smeared with oil. Undaunted, we went aboard. It was now eight in the evening. The inspector of the Mounted Police welcomed us and took us to his cabin. This was Henry Larsen, of Northwest Passage fame, the officer commanding "G" Division of the RCMP. He was a most remarkable individual; his exploits in Arctic waters are part of the history of this country. His native land, Norway, heaped him with honours, but the Canadian Government was very slow to recognize his achievements.

Lake Harbour was our next port of call. At the far side of Frobisher Bay, just by Grinnell Glacier, we spotted a polar bear. It was my first and only encounter with "Nanook of the North" during my five-year stint in the land of the Inuit. The RCMP and I were all set to go ashore and hunt it, but the Inuit strongly advised us to remain on board. A wounded bear is a dangerous quarry. Slowly, we glided in to the far side of the small bay and when within range, we fired. The bear, quite unperturbed, merely turned around and ambled away. For a moment it disappeared behind a series of boulders. When it came into full view again, more shots rang out and the bear leaped into the air. One bullet had found the mark. In amazement, I watched its massive frame hurtling down the mountainside leaving a trail of blood on the snowclad face. As it tumbled onto the rocky ground below, one could hear the thud even at a distance of 80 yards. There it lay, still and motionless. The RCMP had accounted for his first polar bear.

Getting the 2,500-pound colossus on board required both strength and skill. The bear was laid out on the deck and well lashed on. The coat was very disappointing: the hair was long and straggly with a decidedly yellowish tinge. One always pictures polar bears as gleaming white. This was a summer pelt which accounted for the discolouring; the March coats are best: short, thick, glossy and creamy white. In spite of the poor quality fur it could still serve as a groundsheet. Because their lives depended entirely upon the basics for survival with no luxuries of any kind, the Inuit had long ago learned to appreciate all that nature afforded. They wasted nothing - a good object lesson for most of us today, living, as we do, with "throwaway" commodities.

Christmas Day on Baffin Island

At the beginning of December I left Lake Harbour for a short trip, intending to return before Christmas. On the third day the lake ice reasonably close to shore began to crack. The dogs, sensing danger, stopped. My guide, Matthew, jumped off the sled and went forward to test the ice. Using a long-handled ice pick, he tapped the ice and concluded that it was safe enough to cross. The dogs knew better. Presently, we crashed through and found ourselves standing knee-deep in water. Crawling onto the ice, we rubbed snow on our legs to absorb as much water as possible. No damage was done. Following a consultation, we decided to risk it a second time. Shortly, the dogs pulled up again. We trod warily and on reaching the lead dog, plunged through once more. We gave up in despair and turned the team homeward. On our way back, I collected Arctic willows, the only semblance of a shrub in this stark land. I planned to use them as Christmas decorations.

Homecoming

In the early hours of December 22nd, the first dog team of the season could be seen in the far distance slowly picking its way across the ice to our little settlement. Many minutes passed before the moving object began to take shape. Now we could see it quite clearly. The leading team had arrived in the harbour and was crossing the ice barrier which skirts the shoreline. Then came another, and another and yet another - all converging on Lake Harbour. Soon, the little hamlet sleeping peacefully in the grip of an Arctic winter suddenly came to life. Tents sprang up like mushrooms, hastily erected for short-term accommodation, and the rounds of visiting began. The Inuit families, temporarily abandoning their winter shelters, had come to share the joys of Christmas with us. They had come from far and wide, within a radius of a few hundred miles.

Several days prior to the invasion, the nurse, Mildred Decker, and school teacher, Isobel Erickson, and I were busily engaged making preparations for a concert which was held for the benefit of the community. We made paper flowers, stage curtains and a Christmas tree - all under the supervision of Isobel. She was very innovative and had lots of good ideas.

The church was decorated for the occasion. The homemade Christmas tree was a work of art. An old broom handle, studded with holes, served as the trunk and the willows, wrapped in green crepe paper with frilled edges, provided the branches. These, in turn, were festooned with paper flowers, streamers, red bows, and candles. The completed masterpiece stood in a prominent place in the church for all to behold. Clusters of tender willow sprigs, with red bows, hung from the retable - a shelf at the back of the altar used for supporting lights and ornaments. The windowsills were decorated with candles and paper flowers. The overall effect was quite stunning.

The Midnight Eucharist

The service was scheduled for eleven-thirty the night before Christmas. The hour was for the benefit of the white settlers. The Inuit do not regulate their lives by the clock; they eat when they are hungry and sleep when they are tired.

The church bell rang out over the landscape calling all to worship. In the pale evening light, I could see the flaps of the tents being thrown open, small figures tumbling out and making their way, lanterns in hand, to the wooden church appropriately situated in the heart of the settlement overlooking the harbour. The weather was cold and brumal, but that did not deter them. I stood by the door, above which hung a storm lantern shedding its red glow across the threshold.

The first arrivals occupied the pews at the rear. They did not sit in families; the men and boys sat on one side and the women, girls and small children on the other. Infants were carried on their mother's backs. When these babies began to cry, breast-feeding was the stopper.

By the time the white people arrived, the only vacant pews were at the front. The group of six was a little hesitant about coming forward so I guided them up the aisle. Their attendance meant much to me and to the Inuit. And there wasn't an Anglican among them. That wonderful spirit of friendship and goodwill, manifest in every part of the north, was much in evidence. There was no barrier of race, colour, language, or creed. What a lesson in tolerance for our fractured world.

The stove was going full blast, the pipes a roseate hue, tree and windowsill candles glowing. Six aladdin lanterns hanging from the ceiling gave light and warmth as the service began.

The Inuit are, by nature, somewhat reserved. This characteristic is very evident in the presence of white people; Anglicans, for the most part, are God's frozen people. I decided, by way of introduction, to have a singsong to thaw out the congregation. The post manager's wife played the breathless harmonium. The opening carols were a feeble effort, but gradually the warming process was beginning to take effect. Soon, we all got into the swing of it and were belting out hymns at the top of our voices. On this note, the Eucharist proper began.

The service, of course, was in Inuktitut. The homily, for the benefit of those who could not understand the Inuit tongue, was given in both languages. At the conclusion, I stood at the door and shook hands with everybody, wishing each a Merry Christmas. I watched crouched forms, with lighted lanterns, shuffling along the narrow pathway. Inside each tent, the lantern was hung up and the black kettle filled with lumps of ice and put on the primus stove. The Inuit were about to have a night-cap: a cup of strongly brewed tea. Tobacco and papers were rolled into cigarettes for the ultimate luxury. As I left the church, tents were aglow in a fairyland, far from the trappings of the civilized world. I joined my companions at the nursing station for our night-cap: coffee and cake. We sat chatting until three in the morning.

Christmas Dinner and Concert

It was decided to have our Christmas dinner at midday. A dress rehearsal was essential for the concert which was scheduled to take place in the evening. Mildred and Isobel prepared a delicious meal. Food-wise it was a community effort. The meal was served at the mission house, as the nursing station was too small to seat everybody comfortably. There were several courses. The menu: tomato juice, soup, roast beef - the post manager had reserved one so that we would have fresh meat at Christmas - dehydrated potatoes, corn, asparagus,

Christmas pudding, cake and coffee. Quite a repast, one must admit, for those living in isolation.

The concert took place in the HBC warehouse where the Inuit had helped to clear the floor of oil drums, crates and cartons, and to erect a makeshift stage. Lanterns were hung from the ceiling and the Christmas tree installed to create a festive atmosphere.

Geordie Anderson, the post manager, acted as MC. He had spent more years in the north than all of us put together, and could speak the Inuit language quite fluently. He greeted the audience and welcomed them to the evening's entertainment.

We opened the proceedings with the singing of the National Anthem accompanied on the harmonium by Geordie's wife, Mrs. A. For some unknown reason, his wife was always referred to as "Mrs. A." Geordie could not persuade any of the Inuit to play the piano accordion although many were very proficient.

The singing of several carols gave a Christmas flavour to the occasion. The trial run on Christmas Eve had strengthened vocal cords. Next was an Irish folk dance, "Saturday Night," performed by four of the school children. Isobel had taught them the various steps, which for little girls were rather difficult, but they acquitted themselves very well indeed. Everyone present was most surprised, particularly the Inuit, who at the end of the act clapped so long that an encore was inevitable. Geordie asked, "Would you like more?" With one voice came the reply: "Elale" ("Yes, indeed"). So the children repeated the act and the response was equally enthusiastic. It was obvious that the audience was clamouring for a third, but Geordie stepped in and announced the next item on the programme: a puppet show by Mildred and Deck, the junior RCMP. It was the most sophisticated performance of the evening and very cleverly executed.

One more act before intermission: a shadowgraph by the children. A sheet was hung across the stage and by means of backlighting, the shadows were depicted on the sheet. The music was to the tune of "John Brown's Body" and the white population formed the choir. We composed our own words - lost in the mists of time, I'm afraid - bearing on the life of the country. There were ten stanzas written and sung in English, Geordie interpreting each verse. When the music stopped, the children enacted the scene. We had now reached the halfway mark. The intermission gave us a breather.

Geordie, who had served the Company in numerous Arctic posts, had some eight-millimetre movies of the country. Unfortunately, the bulb blew as the first few feet of the film were in progress. He had no spare. Much to the disappointment of all, we were left in the dark. Unflappable Geordie improvised: he inveigled a small group of Inuit, picked at random, to give us a musical number. It was like drawing teeth, but Geordie managed to encourage some to come forward. Very wisely, he persuaded a noted piano accordion player and a drummer - the drum was a piece of caribou skin tightly stretched over a wooden hoop - to accompany the singers. Some of the older men and women seemed likely candidates. The post manager, mentioning some by name, asked them and the musicians to come on stage. They sang some very haunting melodies from their inherited repertoire. They gave a very creditable performance - and without the benefit of a rehearsal. The prolonged applause was most fitting. Not to be outdone, the two RCMPs and I countered with a few songs. None of us could sing at all, but the audience was thrilled and called for an encore. We agreed, and took another stab at it, apparently keeping them spellbound.

In keeping with the tenor of the season, "Jingle Bells" was sung by everybody, in Inuktitut and in English, as Santa Claus appeared in full regalia. Deck played the part to perfection. He entered rubbing his hands, and explained in Inuktitut how cold it was and what a nasty trip he had had. He shook hands with all the children and gave each a tiny bag of candy. This brought the concert to an end. But more was in store; we could not possibly send them home without something to eat. Geordie asked them to go back to their tents and return with plates, mugs and cutlery for the sumptuous feast.

A washtub, the largest container available, was filled to capacity with meat - mostly seal - plus canned beans, vegetables, dehydrated potatoes, macaroni, raisins, sultanas, rice, and several cartons of cornstarch. What a concoction! The guests lined up and a ladleful was scooped onto each plate. It went down well. The second course: a tub of Jello, with dried figs and apricots to add to the flavour. Third course: tea and hardtack biscuits.

It was a day the Inuit of Lake Harbour will long remember. One could not help but notice the expressions on their faces. Like their oriental cousins, they can be rather inscrutable, but on this Christmas Day they had dropped the mask and thoroughly enjoyed the day's fun. The thought that they had left the building thoroughly satisfied with the entertainment, to say nothing of the repast, fully compensated us for the time involved in the preparations. Next morning, they had all departed for their hunting grounds. The little hamlet was quite deserted once more.

Winter Quarters on the Barren Lands

During my years in the Arctic, the Inuit did not live in settlements as we know them. They travelled in to Lake Harbour to sell fur and buy supplies, but the campsite was determined by the availability of seal meat and would therefore be reasonably close to the floe edge. All families were dependent upon fur from the traplines as their source of income, so a balance had to be struck in location between meat and fur.

Winter igloos are built to last an entire winter and are, therefore, much more elaborate and considerably larger than a trail snow house. The number of igloos varies from camp to camp. A single-igloo camp is not a rarity, but might easily give the impression that the family had been ostracised, which is not the case. The Inuit live a very communal life and depend upon one another for their very existence. One household might be inundated with visitors just to make sure that all is well. There is a rule of thumb which is strictly adhered to: the amount of food available in any given area will govern the size of the camp. Within reason, the more abundant the wildlife the greater the number of hunters. Families will usually return to the same hunting grounds year after year.

Dogsleds will adorn the tops of the igloos so that the sealskin lashings are out of reach of animals. Similarly, the dogs' traces, neatly spiralled, can be seen hanging from a pole. Sealskins, the blubber scraped off with an ulu, are draped over a line; while others, tightly stretched over a semicircular, wooden framework, will be hung up to dry. All skins are frost-cured. One also comes upon small sleds by igloo doors, primarily for the children's use. The son of the household can often be seen sitting side-saddle, contemplating the day when he can take part in the chase. On clear days, he will take off over the ice with a few dogs just to get the feel of things. His father will give him a few pointers from time to time, and before reaching his majority the boy will be a reasonably competent driver and handler of a team.

Dogs are much in evidence, wandering about the camp ever in search of food. Rations are in short supply between trips. Marauding animals are not likely to invade a camp where dogs are present. Paddles, harpoons, kayaks - usually resting on tripods - are pertinent reminders of the Inuit way of life.

It is time to pay a visit to one of the dwellings. It actually consists of three igloos, standing shoulder to shoulder and leading one into the other.

The first, and smallest, is reserved mainly for the dogs. On bitterly cold, blustery days the animals pile in and huddle together. A fight always ensues; the more aggressive will commandeer the choice places in the centre of the pack for greater warmth. They are not allowed to occupy the entire floor; there must be no obstruction leading to the door of the second igloo. To avoid this, a trough, enclosed by a snow wall, is constructed on the right-hand side for their use and woe betide the husky found loitering outside the restricted area. The door, a block of snow, has been permanently removed to allow easy access back and forth.

Crawling on hands and knees, we enter. The dogs, resting quietly, pay little attention to us. Making our way across the floor, we come to the second igloo. Here, we reach a door about two feet, six inches in height, made from wooden crates or driftwood, which serves a most important function: the dog food is stored in this area and the frame door bars entry. Indeed all supplies, including human, are cached here, so that one can see at a glance whether the Inuit are experiencing a feast or a famine. Move forward so that you can savour the flavour and atmosphere of the dwelling and share an unforgettable experience. Bend down and be prepared for a shock as you enter: the aroma floats up like a miasma. Its pungent smell will bring tears to the eyes and permeate one's entire being. It is a combination of unwashed bodies, rancid seal oil, blubber and oil-smeared garments. But I had the perfect antidote: perfume!

In my early days, I found the odour so overwhelming that I carried a small bottle of perfume on the trail and dabbed my beard liberally with the precious fragrance before entering an igloo. On one occasion, an Inuk appeared from nowhere and caught me in the act. I am sure he thought that I was having a "quick one," but he would have been much too polite to comment!

Standing with one's back to the entrance, one can see the immensity of the structure. The centre of the floor to the tip of the dome can reach ten feet and the diameter anywhere up to 12 feet. It is a camp effort and has taken days to complete. Igloo building is normally done by men. There are many equally competent women in the field, but they would never dream of offering their services unless asked to do so.

While all igloos are constructed along the same lines, there is a notable difference between an overnight igloo and the winter's permanent living quarters. The former rises rather abruptly, whereas the slope in the latter is much more gradual. In fact, the larger the igloo the more gentle the tapering becomes. When a trail igloo begins to melt, drips descend onto the bedding and when the water becomes a real problem, a pot is used to contain it. Conversely, the dome of the camp igloo is so oblique that the resulting water will run down the sides of the snow wall. This may not be very evident in early winter, but becomes unmistakably clear by spring. One can literally hear the running water and follow its course down the channels, or grooves, caused by the constant flow. Occasionally, the odd drip will appear. An ulu will be used to gouge out the offending bump and smooth things over. The dark shading on the walls will be caused by the occasional smoke from the blubber lamp. Even those who are experienced in handling the lamps can never completely overcome the problem. One must not forget the air hole in the dome. This is essential; bodies and the blubber lamp will generate heat so the warm air must be allowed to escape. Were it unable to find an outlet somewhere, the heat would eventually melt the entire snow house.

Directly opposite the door, and occupying about two-thirds of the floor space, is the sleeping platform. It, too, is made from snow blocks and stands approximately three feet in height. The bed is overlaid with bear and caribou skins, the fur uppermost. On it the family sit, recline, sleep and have their meals. Some may prefer to be seated on the edge, with legs dangling. Eiderdown sleeping bags are tossed on top. The family will sleep with feet towards the wall, the warmest position. Beds are never made; any time can be sleeping time or meal time.

At one extremity of the platform is the blubber lamp where the mother of the family sits, cross-legged, in full command. Above the kudlik (lamp) is the drying rack. It is usually filled to overflowing with duffel mitts, socks, parkas, mukluks and koolituks. It is a very simple structure: two poles are embedded horizontally in the snow wall, their free ends pulled together to form a V, the apex of which is supported by a securely tied vertical pole from the floor. Sealskins lines are strapped, criss-crossing, to hold the garments. A frozen seal will be propped against the wall, with an ulu (knife) nearby. Any member of the family, or a stranger for that matter, can slice off a piece of meat when feeling peckish. Permission is never sought; the Inuit do not stand on ceremony. Rather than cut the meat into small pieces, the chunk is held between the teeth and a razor-sharp ulu severs a mouthful - leaving the lips intact. Many a time have I seen this delicate operation and continue to be amazed at the way in which the tool is so deftly wielded.

The window, inserted into the wall, is a block of ice which not only allows light to filter through, but also acts as a barometer. No need to roll out of the downy couch onto the floor, remove the door and peep outside to see what the weather is like. The window holds the key: if it is clear, all is well; if it is hazy, the day is not suitable for hunting so there is no need to get up!

A Day in the Life of the Inuit

The following depicts domestic practices common enough in the 1940s and '50s, but probably with little relevance to Inuit life today. Obviously, encroaching civilization has altered conditions drastically, and the result is a gradual erosion of unique native skills developed over many centuries. My use of the present tense is not intended to indicate that such family situations exist today, but rather only to record old customs and traditions as I saw them. To me, it is sad that a way of life is now passing - one which we may never see again.

One hears a great deal today about the extended family. Such a concept is normal practice in the Arctic; for centuries this way of life has played a unique role among our native peoples. Mothers and daughters-in-law live in perfect harmony, but within the igloo itself the chief hunter's wife is the dominant figure. Her word is law.

She wears her parka at all times. Safely tucked in the hood is the youngest infant. We see its small head and chubby cheeks, and its dark eyes peering out. The child is sometimes naked. I shall leave the rest to your imagination.

The mother is an indefatigable worker. There is always something to do: mending, sewing, cleaning, scraping sealskins and preparing food. The tools of her trade are the needle, caribou sinew thread, and the ulu - a semicircular metal blade with a T-shaped handle, often of ivory.

The matriarch presides at the kudlik, or blubber lamp. It is carved from steatite (popularly called soapstone because it is relatively easy to carve) which varies in colour from light grey to dark green. In shape, the kudlik resembles a boat cut in half lengthwise. The hull, or depression, is filled with seal oil, and caribou moss crumbs line the straight edge. It works along the same principle as an oil lamp: the wick, in this case the moss, soaks up the oil and is set alight. The lamp burns day and night. To a large extent, the wider the wick the more heat it will generate. When the family has retired for the night, the heat is turned down by reducing the width of the wick with a stick. If properly regulated, it will burn throughout the silent hours. An untrimmed wick will cause an oil lamp to smoke. The same applies to a kudlik; to prevent it from smoking requires the hand of experience. Sometimes the lamp has a flat bottom, like a scow, so that it can sit without danger of spilling the oil. More often than not, it rests on two U-shaped blocks of soapstone, one at either end, and thus can be easily tilted when the oil burns low. The blubber lamp is made by the man, but once presented to his wife it becomes her sole property.

Preparing meals is a simple matter. The pot on the hob is rarely empty; a bannock sizzling in oil, a seal stew or caribou meat in preparation. The Inuit find it difficult to understand why the white man insists upon having meals at appointed hours. Inuit just eat when they are hungry.

The setting of a table is unheard of and would be totally impracticable in a snow house. Households are never cluttered with unnecessary furniture. Besides, it would be most unlikely that everyone would be hungry at the same time. All meals are moveable feasts. Continuous snacks are the order of the day.

When the eldest son marries, he brings his bride to the family igloo. The matriarch will gladly share some of the household duties with her daughter-in-law. After years of chewing skins and mukluks, the elder's teeth may be worn to the point where chewing causes great discomfort, so the newest member of the family will be pressed into service.

A traumatic change takes place when the patriarch passes on; the domestic mantle now falls to the son's wife. The widow, the deposed ruler, no longer has any authority and accepts with equanimity her lost status. She will recede into the background and the younger woman will assume her rightful place at the blubber lamp. The widow will assist with the daily chores. She would never be considered a charity case. The Inuit family is a closely knit unit and its members depend upon one another for survival; each has a contribution to make. Indeed, in days gone by when an ageing father felt that he could no longer contribute to the general welfare and was becoming a liability, he would walk out into the Arctic night. The family might well be aware of his intention, but not a word would be spoken. His mind would have been made up and nothing would, or could, be done about it. His body, or what remained of it, would be recovered in the spring and given honourable burial.

"Wife swapping" was a reasonably common practice and, as a missionary, I was sometimes expected to make a moral judgement. One could not deny that it took place, even in the mid-1940s, but it hadn't always a sexual connotation. In some instances, sex played a very minor role in the exchange. Sometimes it was done for the most practical of reasons. An Inuk living in the bush country might like to spend a winter in the barren lands. In order to do so, he would be required, for such was their moral code, to make the necessary arrangements with his tundra counterpart. The respective wives would not be consulted; they would simply be expected to fall in with the plan. The bush country wife would be hopelessly at sea in the tundra; tending a blubber lamp would be quite foreign to her. The tundra wife, on the other hand, would find conditions very different in the bush, but would be able to cope more readily; stuffing a wood stove is scarcely mind-boggling. She would, however, find it hard to adjust to the rise and fall of the temperature, and the flimsy tent, compared with the solid igloo, would afford little protection. She would long for the glow and steady warmth of the kudlik.

Situations like this resulted in wife exchanges on a temporary basis. This may sound less shocking today than it did fifty years ago considering the morals of the present time, but Inuit fathers, unlike many in our so-called civilized society, had no desire to escape their responsibilities. Any children born of such a temporary union were always lovingly cared for; amicable arrangements would be made for their future welfare.

The Inuit adore children and they are given free rein. Very rarely is a child reprimanded and never spanked - shades of Dr. Spock! One of the few restrictions is to keep them indoors when it is snowing and blowing. A sudden snow drift could swallow them up in record time. Under favourable weather conditions, regardless of the cold, the older children will play out-of-doors. A popular sport is "spiking the can." An empty tin is placed on the snow and the contestants line up in order, at a reasonable distance from the target, and take aim. The spear is a harpoon with the barb removed. The purpose of the game is to see which competitor can account for the most strikes.

Another pastime for teenagers is learning how to handle a dog team. The average sled would be too cumbersome for novices so a smaller variety is used for the purpose. The runners are shod with mud - fathers will oversee the preparation and shoeing - and a main trace attached. Harnessing the dogs is a simple task and one the teenagers have seen since childhood. Three or four dogs are hitched up, a driver takes his seat at the helm and all available spaces are soon occupied. On a given order, they are on their way across the barren wastes. The dogs are not controlled by reins; they obey commands.

Strictly speaking, the only trained member of the team is the lead dog. It takes the initiative, is the most intelligent and quite often the most dominant animal. When a teenager can handle a team with ease, several more huskies will be added. Among the number may be a new recruit. Harnessed and hitched for the first time, it will be an interesting experience for dog and driver alike. The animal will "take off in all directions." A sudden jolt of the trace will have a salutary effect: be dragged along or join the pack. Soon it will get the message and cooperate. In course of time, the driver will graduate to a full-blown team and sled. By the time he is ready to accompany his father on a trip, he will be able to manage a team with the utmost confidence.

Life may be more leisurely in the Arctic, but the danger of starvation is an ever-present threat, hanging over the household for much of the year. Essentially it is the reason they are a semi-nomadic people. If one were to enter an igloo when the food supply is at a low ebb, the visitor would be warmly welcomed and offered the usual fare. To all outward appearances, the occupants wouldn't have a worry in the world, but the perceptive caller would not be so easily deceived. There would be no reference to the lack of food, but the situation would be rectified as soon as possible.

On good days, there will be a sealing expedition to the sea ice. In the spring, the Inuit spend countless hours on the saltwater ice in search of game. They have endless patience and will pass entire days, if need be, stalking their elusive quarry.

A seal's breathing hole is not private property. Many seal will use the same opening and help to keep it free of ice. This is not too difficult in the early part of winter; the thin layer of ice can be cracked without much effort. However, as the days wear on and the temperature drops considerably, it becomes much more difficult. Here, the seal must scratch and bite the ice until daylight appears. The diameter of the hole is larger at the base of the ice which gives the animal more working space. This bell-shaped opening enables the seal to flex its muscles for the leap upwards. Like all mammals, they must come up for air frequently. They push their snouts through the broken fragments and survey the scene. When assured that the coast is clear, they propel themselves through the hole and rest their front flippers on the ledge. A final lunge and they emerge from the deep. One often wonders how many run out of breath before the hole is cleared. And how do seal find these holes in the first place - particularly in subzero weather when the snow lies thick and heavy above?

During the long, sunny days of spring, seal can be seen sunning themselves on the ice. They look an easy target, but for a hunter to get within range is much more difficult than one might imagine. The concealing device is a white screen, a piece of drill or cotton, the fabric tightly stretched over a wooden frame, with a peephole at eye level. Holding the shield in front of him with one hand, and carrying his rifle with the other, the hunter moves, wormlike, towards his prey. When within range the first shot rings out. The black specks on the ice disappear in a flash. If the shot has found its mark, the hunter will rush forward to claim his booty before it struggles into the breathing hole and is lost forever.

In stalking a seal, a stealthy approach to the breathing hole is paramount. Seal have acute hearing so the slightest movement on the crunchy snow will indicate danger. The Inuk waits patiently for his cue: as the mammal moves towards the breathing hole, it emits a blowing sound which is the signal for the hunter to advance. By fits and starts, the hole is finally reached. Here the hunter stands motionless with the harpoon in the firing position. When he hears the seal, he will estimate its time of arrival and plunge the spear, hopefully into the skull. It is all a matter of timing. If successful, he must now land the kill. The hole has to be enlarged. Meanwhile the seal is straining at the line and has to be reeled in from time to time. A gaff is often used to extricate it.

Children will learn from their parents all the necessary skills to equip themselves for later life. It will be a joint effort. An Inuit man and his wife form a partnership. Each has a contribution to make and each is dependent upon the other. Mothers will teach their daughters and fathers their sons. Friendly rivalry of eager students promotes interest in the lessons given by the parents. The classes are not structured. No notes are taken, but the pupils, the very epitome of decorum, listen intently to the instruction and follow every intricate detail of the work at hand. Like their elders, they appear to have photographic minds. Once shown an image, they can call it up at will.

How hunters find the time to teach their offspring the fundamentals remains a mystery, but they will teach every facet of Arctic life and survival. It will take many years of continuous training. There is a regular litany of arts and crafts to be mastered: the making and fashioning of sleds, blubber lamps, kayaks, harpoons and bow drills; igloo building; and, of course, hunting and fishing. The list goes on. Soapstone carvers will pass on the art to those who show promise. Ivory carvings, much in vogue in the 1940s, are rarely seen today. They were discontinued possibly for ecological considerations. Elephants in Africa, as we well know, were slaughtered wholesale for their tusks. The Inuit would never resort to that kind of behaviour. Having worked and lived with them, I am well aware of a hunter's sound judgement.

Daughters will be given an excellent grounding in every aspect of clothing, the dressing of skins and sewing of komiks for summer and winter wear. I often saw beautiful examples of elaborate beadwork, and generally all women were skilled with the needle. Dolls are the homespun variety: their clothing a copy, on a small scale, of everyday wear.

There are times when a project will involve the whole family. The construction and waterproofing of a kayak is a good example. The man will cut, shape and assemble the framework. His wife will prepare the seal skins, drape them over the kayak and sew them together making the craft completely watertight, although all are pieced together with needle and sinew. The skins are sewn on wet and limp and tighten as they dry out. Some are more elastic than others, so allowances must be made. It all looks very simple, but the hands of experts are at work.

Adrift on an Ice Pan

In spite of the brevity of an Arctic summer, I spent many weeks in boats or canoes during the warmer weather. Dog teams still remained my passion, and by August a sort of reverse cabin fever had usually set in. Winter travel had proved to be the best way of keeping in touch with my semi-nomadic congregation; it gave me, at the same time, an opportunity to see as much of the country as possible.

Late in the year, I left Lake Harbour for Cape Dorset - a small Inuit settlement about 250 miles northwest. The purpose of the exercise was to visit a number of isolated encampments which were dotted along the coastline. We were fortunate to reach our destination at all. Crossing shore ice onto a lake, Moses, my guide, pulled up the team to get his bearings and check the ice. The hour of darkness had long overtaken us, but the moon, wan though it was, helped us to see the way ahead.

There was very little snow on the lake and the sled kept sliding at an angle. It was very difficult for Moses to steer it in the right direction. We stopped several times as a safety precaution to test the ice. Moses used the pointed shaft of a harpoon. Occasionally, he would drop to one knee and peer through the ice. Flashlights don't function too well in subzero weather, so he had to resort to matches. Once he left me in charge of the team. Hen-toed and with crouched gait, he shuffled along and eventually disappeared. All kinds of thoughts ran through my mind. Had the dogs suddenly taken off, for example, I could not have controlled them. I had visions of the ice giving way and my being swept underneath.

Such chilling thoughts galvanized me into action. I grabbed the whip and cracked it regularly while standing at the head of the team. Little did they know that I was a complete novice in the field, unable to take command in the usual way. But I must have looked the part. One dog came a little too close for comfort, so I gave it a swat on the nose. The brute swore at me. The Inuit treat their dogs well. Occasionally, a driver will show little mercy and use the lash to good effect. This may sound cruel, but at that time an Inuk was totally dependent upon his team for transportation, indeed his livelihood. Dogs were not pets; they formed a working partnership with their master. A good team was a highly prized possession and a first-rate driver had his dogs under perfect control. He was the envy of the entire camp.

To my great relief, Moses returned. I could see that all was not well. He said that a strip of open water lay ahead - another river perhaps - or it may have been the continuation of the river which led us onto the lake in the first place. But there was a brighter side: an Inuit camp was on the horizon. We retraced our steps and stopped once more. Alone again, Moses took off and continued to strike matches as he trudged along. I stood quietly by, the dogs resting. Vaguely, I thought that I could hear trickling water. Putting my ear to the ice, there was no doubt in my mind. I drew Moses's attention to it upon his return. His comment was as graphic as it was unexpected. Loosely translated: "Let's get the hell out of here."

Very gingerly, we moved away and made for shore. Suddenly, and to the amazement of man and beast, we crashed through the ice. About half the sled was submerged. Moses was thrown headlong onto the ice and I was catapulted into the frigid water. Recovering, Moses rushed to my assistance, saw that my head and shoulders were above water, and promptly disappeared!

My koolituk was acting as a sort of life preserver, so I was not in danger of drowning - only freezing to death. To put it mildly, I was astonished. Admittedly, he returned in a matter of almost seconds. On more sober reflection, however, I could understand the wisdom of his action: he went to check the sled. Had the ice under the runners given way, all could have been lost. Meanwhile, I tried to extricate myself. My limbs were getting more numb by the second. I was unable to lift myself out of the water and crawl onto the ice. Moses, kneeling on the edge of the cavity, wrapped the whip under my arms and hauled me to safety. Standing on the lake, he had to act swiftly. In mere seconds my clothing would have resembled a coat of armour. He removed my koolituk and literally stripped me to my underwear, giving me a vigorous rubdown. Moving quickly, he helped to dress me in dry clothing which he had ferreted out from the dunnage bag. Caribou and polar bear skins had kept things remarkably dry. It is amazing what the human frame can withstand when put to the test.

Wasting little time, we set our course for the shore. I could still manoeuvre awkwardly. To get my circulation going again, I hobbled alongside the sled for the greater part of the journey. Within an hour we had reached the welcome of the campsite and help was at hand to dry out my frozen garments.

How lucky we were not to find ourselves building a trail igloo after such an experience. We both began to relax, feeling that the worst of our journey might be behind us. If fortune was smiling at last, its blessing was to be brief indeed.

My wife tells me that years ago, in the *Ontario School Reader*, there was a story called "Adrift on an Ice Pan." It was a harrowing tale. I can well believe it; it happened to me.

In the mid-1940s in the eastern Arctic, all winter travelling was done by dog team. Under normal conditions, when food was beginning to run out at a camp, the men might decide to go to the floe edge to replenish the larder. Teenagers, champing at the bit, always hoped that they might be among the chosen and asked to go along. Some would be fortunate and go for the experience, but only a limited number.

The day of departure is never pre-arranged. The Inuit don't plan things in advance. This may sound strange to our ears, but perfectly understandable from their point of view. When the right day comes, the leading hunter, or the "camp boss" as he is called, gives the order, the teams are mobilised and the contingent moves at high speed to the hunting grounds. A spare sled will be used to haul the canoe or kayak.

Sealing at the floe edge is a popular endeavour, but the Inuit would never refer to it as a "sport." Sealing, while enjoyable, is strictly business and can become a matter of life and death. The Inuit never kill animals indiscriminately, only in sufficient quantity to ward off the pangs of hunger for a few days and not a season. There still lingers an ancient superstition that the soul of a dead seal might appear and seek retribution for unwarranted slaughter.

If the wind is blowing inland, so much the better; the maimed mammals will drift in towards the margin of the ice and can easily be picked up. As they are well insulated with blubber, there is little danger of losing them. When the wind is blowing out to sea, the technique is somewhat different. Here it is necessary to use the canoe, or kayak, to collect the bag and tow it to the ice shelf. Standing at the floe edge in

January or February at -50°F is not really my idea of fun. It is a cold and often frustrating experience, but a necessary one.

Conditions were very different on that overcast day when my guide and I set out for the floe edge. We were alone and not members of a hunting party. We had neither canoe nor kayak and were dependent upon the wind, frequently variable and uncertain. On this occasion it was in our favour: blowing in towards the ice on which we were standing. But the tide was also a factor.

Bad weather and poor travelling conditions had impeded our progress greatly. We were several days behind schedule and our food supply was at a minimum which forced us to do something about the situation. We had been moving along the sea ice, a much travelled thoroughfare, so the floe edge was not too far afield.

Seal were not too plentiful and a few hours elapsed before we could claim one. It was the only kill of the day. By the time we were ready to leave the scene and return to our igloo we discovered, to our horror, that we were unable to retrace our steps; the large pan on which we were standing had come adrift from the main shore ice and we were moving out to sea. It was quite impossible to span the yawning crevasse, nor were we able to throw the dogs over. The wind was beginning to change direction, which complicated matters. Moses was very philosophical about the whole situation, but I did not share his optimism. I asked him what we should do. "Nothing," was his immediate response. I pressed him further. "Well," he said, "if the wind changes we shall get back; if not, we won't." Some consolation! With that, he sat down on the seal and pulled some tobacco out of his pocket, rolled a cigarette and lighted it. His calm acceptance of our plight illustrates the Inuit stoical attitude towards life.

While his comments were far from encouraging, his fortitude in the face of mortal danger made any outward display of inner panic morally impossible. I was, after all, his spiritual adviser, and if he could face death with such equanimity how could I do less? Christian belief demanded Christian example and here was an opportunity to match mine with his.

It is difficult to put into words the thoughts which raced through my mind. There was always the possibility that the pan might break up and that we would be stranded on a smaller one. The farther we drifted out to sea, the greater the probability of disaster. We moved in to the team and stayed close together. Rough seas could have been our undoing and put an end to it all.

Exactly how long we were cruising among the floes, I cannot now recall. It was several hours and too long for comfort! Had the wind not changed direction, I would not be here to relate the experience. Darkness had long enshrouded us by the time we reached the shelter and security of the snow house. Never before had I looked upon an igloo as comfortable quarters. Times and attitudes change.

From Feast to Famine

While it may appear that most of my Arctic travelling was confined to the Ungava area, in actual fact I spent an equal amount of time on the trail each year when based on Baffin Island.

During the winter of 1950-51, my diary records that in common with the previous years I was continually on the move from camp to camp visiting the Inuit and taking services. I left the mission house at Lake Harbour in mid-December, heading for Frobisher Bay where I was to spend Christmas. Apart from two weeks in February, I was away from home for over three months.

December was not always the best month for travel and this year there seemed to be less snow than on my previous trips, at least at the beginning. On this occasion another team accompanied us: one of the RCMP was making his rounds but needed some help with the language. A few sleeps from Frobisher we encountered a small falls almost swept clear by gale force winds. We made several attempts on the ascent, but the almost perpendicular ice wall proved too formidable. The guides even doubled the length of the bridles - which allowed the dogs to get a footing on the snow rather than the glare ice - but still no progress was made. We then dragged the sled backwards, angling it to one side, shooed the dogs into position and attacked a steep hill on the left bank. After much hauling and pulling we got both sleds up and then took a snakelike course to avoid the rocks, coming down finally to the top of the falls. Although the height was scarcely ten feet the operation had taken two hours. Both teams and men were exhausted so we built in for the night.

Next day we made a slow start, breaking camp about ten o'clock. The snow was well packed on this side of the falls and we made good time. By noon, Akavak's team was pulling away from ours and by half-past three he wanted to stop. I pressed him to go on and we continued together for another hour. The moon again helped us no end - darkness had already fallen. The cold was intense, but the northern lights were spectacular. I tried to photograph them while the igloo was being built.

The following day produced mixed weather conditions. The wind had again changed to the south and very fine snow, feeling more like minute particles of hail, stung our faces for most of the morning. Before the day finished the wind had switched to the northeast again. We all felt the biting cold. That night there were three primus stoves heating the igloo.

Our party was due to meet a team from Frobisher Bay to complete the journey. Akavak was our main guide, but had only contracted for part of the trip and was now anxious to return home. He agreed to push on for a few more miles in case the fresh team turned up, but then changed his mind leaving Kapik and Thomasi in charge. Neither seemed to be very sure of the route. In fact, Kapik said to me, "We are lost."

"But you told me you knew the way to Frobisher," I retorted.

"The last time I was here." he replied, "it was drifting so hard we could not see a thing." His excuse seemed rather contradictory until I realized that poor visibility had obscured the landmarks, and the terrain was indeed unfamiliar. The wind had changed so frequently that any useful markings on the surface of the snow had not yet been established. The guides held a further conference and I overheard one say, "Akavak is lucky. He is on the way home!"

We struck out again, presently reaching a river which led directly to Frobisher Bay. Weather permitting, we should reach Frobisher the next day and the HBC the following morning. We stopped to build our shelter at six o'clock. Kapik was quite a good builder and reasonably quick. The night passed uneventfully.

We had experienced really good going for the month of December, but finally there was a price to be paid. The snow lay deep on the river and although we were travelling downhill, the dogs found it difficult to draw the sled. At a point where the river widened we stopped for lunch, close to the only patch of glare ice we had seen all day. In spite of the break, the dogs were tiring perceptibly and Kapik and I took turns walking ahead of the team for most of the afternoon. On one of my solo walks I shot three ptarmigan and shortly afterwards, while still breaking trail, I fell through the ice. Fortunately the water was shallow, for here the snow was deepest of all and I floundered through it up to my waist.

With Kapik in the lead, Thomasi and I manned the sled. We soon encountered rough shore ice. It was necessary to unlash the sled partially, and Thomasi went ahead of the dogs waving the ptarmigan to entice them. We moved only two feet at a time, finally reaching land again. The animals were close to exhaustion. In spite of another beautiful moon-swept night it was impossible to continue. Thomasi and I collected our gear and Kapik began to build the night's shelter. Thomasi appeared to be nearly frozen and I was beginning to fear for him. I told him to chink the igloo, thinking it might help him get warmer. He carried on for a short time but then gave up; his hands were just too cold. As soon as possible we got him inside and lighted the primus stove.

We rose early to make a good start, travelling again on the river, about to reach the expanse of Frobisher Bay. The moon was shining, its grey light casting oblique shadows across the rough ice. The morning was very cold, the air completely still. The snow continued deep and no one could ride the sled. About an hour from shore I came across two polar bear tracks, quite fresh and side by side. Here I waited until the team reached me. Kapik thought that they had passed by during the early hours of the morning, or even late last night. After examining the tracks, the guides said the bears were hungry - something about lifting their paws as opposed to dragging them. Often the finer points of their language escaped me and I was not quite sure exactly what they meant. Kapik now took the lead and held it for three hours, then it was my turn. The monotony of this type of travel was incredible. How I hate maowyuk.

At least two hours before reaching our destination, we could see the lights of the HBC. While every step naturally brought us nearer, we certainly did not appear to make any progress. Weary and hungry, we arrived at half-past five. A entire day had been spent covering a distance which last year we had completed in two and a half hours!

I stayed at the HBC post and the next day, which was Christmas Eve, walked over to the Air Base to arrange Christmas services. The OC, the new commanding officer, asked if I would be willing to hold one within a few hours as he was afraid the personnel would be celebrating that night and possibly not at their best by morning! In spite of short notice, there was an excellent attendance. I dropped in to see Bud Johnson, the RCMP, who had set out for Lake Harbour the previous Monday but had been forced back by deep snow.

On Christmas morning I returned to the base for a seven o'clock Eucharist. Despite the OC's misgivings there was a fair congregation. Eight o'clock saw me back at the village for a similar service for the Inuit. The Tolbooms were expecting me to join them for Christmas dinner - two o'clock at the HBC. I had also been invited to the base to share their festivities at a slightly earlier hour. What a meal! We had turkey, ham, fresh vegetables, salad, fresh potatoes, mince pies and Christmas pudding. By midafternoon, a second appetising dinner was on the table and I began to wonder if I would ever make Evensong at seven.

So much food, consumed in such a short time, probably sounds incredibly greedy, but with days and days of scanty trail fare behind me (at night we often settled for hardtack and tea), my appetite was enormous until my body recovered. Extra nourishment also helped to compensate for lack of sleep; travelling conditions seldom promised a restful night.

The next few days were spent writing letters and arranging a tour of Inuit camps. I hired a fresh team and a driver who went by the unusual name of Spyglassie. The weather was mild and cloudy. A strong wind, several days earlier, had helped pack the snow, so travel was much easier and a few hours brought us to Joe's camp. The Inuit had scattered, probably to the floe edge, so we moved along the sea ice hoping to find another group. We came upon some empty tents, unusual in this area, and were forced to make use of one. A storm was brewing and another gale seemed inevitable. The shelter was cold, damp, filthy and miserable; we had hoped to spend only one night, but as the wind howled all the next day, travel was out of the question.

When the weather finally cleared, a short trek brought us to a small camp near Ward Bay. After supper I toured the tents and discovered a sick girl. She was very ill indeed and we made arrangements for her relatives to take her to Frobisher where the base medic could help. The following three weeks were spent in similar fashion - moving from camp to camp. I tried to ensure that each little settlement had equal attention. Even after a long day's travel I would hold at least one service, with possibly a wedding or a baptism as the occasion demanded.

January 23rd, 1951 saw my return to Frobisher where a Canadian Air Force plane had just landed. I was offered a flight to Goose Bay, Labrador, and jumped at the opportunity. We flew by Resolution Island, a desolate spot, where mail was dropped for the staff of the

Department of Transport. Later, I was invited to occupy the copilot's seat where I stayed for half an hour listening to all sorts of technical explanations. It was a beautifully clear night, the visibility excellent.

The RCAF padre had made arrangements for me to stay at the officers' quarters at the Canadian base; the next four days provided a welcome break from my normal routine of dog sled, camps and mission house. Isolation had never really bothered me, but I did enjoy meeting people and the hospitality here was endless. Goose Bay was almost a metropolis compared with Baffin Island. There was even a bus service linking the Canadian and American bases. I was invited to tour the Canadian school where I met the principal and five teachers. The Protestant padre was very hospitable and I had a meal with him at home and met his family. I also ran into his American counterpart at the PX. He invited me to lunch which was very kind. He might have had a slightly ulterior motive - and I really could not have blamed him. He had to give a talk to all the men once a month, Friday at one o'clock in the theatre, and as I was new blood he asked me to fill in. It was all rather impromptu as I had no time to prepare anything. An audience of five hundred can be somewhat overwhelming, particularly to someone who had just spent over four years away from civilization, but I managed.

I had dinner that evening at the Canadian Officers' mess and several of the teachers, who were also present, persuaded me to go to bingo on the American side. An informal dance followed and we caught the late bus home to the teachers' residence where we chatted over coffee until two in the morning.

Saturday, January 26th, was to be my last day at Goose. At intervals, I had been feeling rather tired but had put it down to my late nights and abundance of food. Coffee and sandwiches, even invitations to meals, awaited me everywhere and it was difficult to refuse such kindness. That day I finally realized that I was ill and spent the afternoon lying down. Someone took me to the hospital where the doctor, a very pleasant Irishman, gave me some penicillin and ordered me to rest.

The plane was due to leave the next morning at eight, so I dragged myself out of bed still feeling like death. The heavy snow persisted. No jeeps were available for transport as the roads were impassable. I stepped out the door, plowing through snow to my waist, and in twenty minutes reached the hangar. The aircraft was delayed for an hour, but finally took off in spite of poor visibility. Fortunately, the weather cleared and we arrived at Frobisher without incident. Here the medic insisted that I stay at the base until I was fit to travel. Those few days represented my only brush with illness during five years in the north. I was fortunate to have been at a place where medical attention was at hand.

On February 3rd, I finally left for Lake Harbour with Spyglassie in charge. He was extremely slow about lashing the sled and hitching the dogs. A further delay was necessary because we had to call at his camp, part way across the bay, to pick up an extra man and a second team. We were very heavily laden and remembering the trip before Christmas when the conditions had exhausted the dogs, we wanted extra man- and dog-power. Simonee was already waiting for us with seven dogs, but our progress had been so slow it was too late to move on. Visiting the people while our sleeping bags and gear were being unpacked, I later was horrified to discover that the saw, our sole tool for building a snow house, had somehow dropped off the sled, and my .22 rifle had also disappeared. Spyglassie was evidently not much of a packer.

We broke camp only to face a high wind and a ground drift lasting many hours. The terrain was very rough and the sled upset countless times. Halting in the late afternoon, we had trouble finding suitable snow to build. I chinked the igloo but managed to knock in several blocks - a sure sign the quality was poor. As an extra irritation, we had lost another article: this time my drying rack.

"If we go on at this rate, we shall have a very light load by the time we reach home, still several sleeps distant." [Direct quote from my diary.]

I still had many miles to cover that spring, and visiting the Cape Dorset area remained my next project. My territory was vast and I knew I would be away for a little while to recover my strength. Illness on the trail can be a considerable hazard.

The weeks passed quickly as we moved from place to place. The March weather, often uncertain, was pleasant on the whole and there were many sunny mornings. At midmonth my notes record a day of contrasts. We had been travelling with the smallest team I had ever hired; the animals were slow and seemed in poor condition - a foreshadowing perhaps, of what lay ahead. We came upon the most beautiful igloos I had ever seen, obviously newly built and of unusual design. Three of them had "porches" and the fourth a double porch. All the snow houses had flat roofs, rather like an inverted frying pan. They were absolutely spotless.

We were able to borrow three extra dogs but I had never seen more pathetic beasts. They were walking skeletons; one could almost hear the bones rattle. The food shortage was quite apparent. Their owner had just returned from the floe edge. He had seen no game all day. We were now in the general vicinity of Amadjuak Lake and having trouble with the runners of our sled. The weather was not cold enough for the icing-up which normally took place several times a day and we were losing the mudding. We pulled in to a camp thinking that we might break our journey but here, too, the sealing had been very poor and the people were out of food. Lack of seal did not just spell hunger, it also meant no oil for the blubber lamp and therefore no heat of any kind. We brewed a cup of tea for them and left some supplies. At the next camp, conditions were even worse: the people had been very hungry for several days. The chief hunter was just returning from the floe edge, empty handed once more. We shared our meal with them and again I left supplies. I had not sufficient to see me through to Lake Harbour, but I could not see people hungry.

Pitsulak's camp was only a short distance away, but rough ice forced us to take the long route. My guide kept assuring me that the camp was just around the far point, but in actual fact we passed several points before getting there. Conditions in the camp were quite horrifying. Many of the dogs had perished, leaving only enough for one team. No one had tasted either tea or bannock for ten days. Three of the hunters had left for the floe edge a few days before and were not expected to return soon. Sealing had been almost non-existent and there was little prospect of a catch.

The moment I shook hands with the camp patriarch, in whose tent I was staying, I noticed how thin he was. His wife and sons said he would die any day. He certainly looked very fragile and as I was writing my notes he was lying down moaning pathetically. Beyond comforting the family and feeding the camp the remainder of my supplies, there was little I could do. What I would have given for some of the Christmas fare and the bountiful meals at Goose Bay to soften such tragic conditions, even temporarily!

Just before dark a man returned on foot from the hunt. I saw him sitting on a sled near the tent, weary beyond all description. He had walked an entire day seeing nothing. About ten o'clock another Inuk wandered home. He had shot an Arctic hare. Despite the fact that they had not tasted food for days, they asked me to share it with them.

We were to set off in the early morning and while the sled was being lashed I said goodbye to Pitsulak. The old man roused himself and whispered, "Will you say goodbye to the others for me - the police, the post manager and his wife, and the Inuit? I shall never see them again." His poor wife began to weep. I said some prayers with them and gave him the Church's blessing. It might have seemed little enough in the face of stark tragedy when material help was so desperately needed but one must never underestimate the power of prayer.

Our immediate destination was Shorty's camp. It meant backtracking but we had to find a new team. My food supplies had dwindled to a small amount of tea and I was a good five days from Lake Harbour. We were not likely to come across game for some time - perhaps not at all. Our situation was serious. Fortunately, our arrival was well timed; a hunter had just appeared with a square flipper seal. Knowing we were out of food he generously gave me the liver. We had barely finished supper when a few children ran in to announce that four teams, headed by the police, could be seen on the ice. Constable Donnan had saved the day. Naturally, there was great excitement and rejoicing among the Inuit; on my part considerable relief that I would not be required to travel on tea alone to Lake Harbour.

A widow and her two small boys from Pitsulak's camp struggled in that evening. It had taken them three days to walk and without nourishment of any kind. My heart went out to them; we were so relieved to be able to offer good food at last. I reported the widespread starvation in the area to Donnan who promised to send out further supplies on our return home.

Farewell and Retrospection

The season was summer and the year 1951. My five years in the Arctic were nearly over.

Arrangements had been made for me to return to civilization on the annual supply ship, the *C. D. Howe,* on its return to Lake Harbour from the northern outposts. However, with the captain's permission, I joined the ship immediately on its first visit to our settlement. The prospective trip enabled me to visit the remote ports on Baffin and even cross to Ellesmere Island, where supplies were unloaded. There I took part in a brief ceremony during which the flag was raised to affirm Canada's possession of the Island. The Inuit here were a striking group, in clean parkas, scrubbed and polished to welcome the ship. Their appearance was quite different from any whom I had ever seen. Perhaps in such an isolated area, the blood lines had not mingled to the same degree. Many years later, my wife and I were attending a movie in a local theatre. Prior to the main event, a National Film Board short flashed on the screen. There I was, in full clericals, on Ellesmere Island conducting a brief service at the foot of the flag pole!

During the voyage, the ship held a little celebration - a rather faint imitation of the familiar shipboard gala when crossing the equator. It was a very low-key affair and I was asked to show some of my Arctic slides to vary the entertainment.

In September we dropped anchor at Lake Harbour once more. As usual, the whole settlement came out and I was able to shake hands and say goodbye to everyone present.

I looked forward to the "outside," returning to Ireland and seeing my family again, but my joy was tinged with sadness. I was leaving a people whom I had grown to respect and admire. It was unlikely that any of us would meet again.

People so often say to me, "Whatever possessed you to go to the mission field? You had such a pleasant, comfortable life in Ireland - why would you ever want to leave it?"

I suppose, on deep reflection, I had two reasons which, in combination, represent the duality in a priest's life - the spiritual and the worldly. Obviously, if one believes that Christianity is not just a religion, but *the* way of life, then it is something which one is obliged to share.

My primary purpose in setting out was, quite naturally, a religious one: the spreading of the Christian gospel. I was aware, of course, that I was not going to Christianize a lot of heathen - the Anglican Church first entered the Arctic about midway through the last century - but I was to continue the endeavour which had been started and which might well disappear if not carried on. I had a genuine commitment to missionary work and did not look upon it as an ordeal, but rather a privilege.

I would be less than honest, however, if I did not admit that my missionary zeal was probably encouraged by a young man's love of adventure. This side of my makeup, far from being a handicap, was to prove invaluable; it challenged me to reach areas almost inaccessible and to accept untold risks and dangers. This is an example of one side of a priest's life complementing the other. For me, the Arctic was the ideal proving ground for my two natures to work together in perfect unison. There was no struggle for domination - each was satisfied.

As a bachelor, it was easy for me to commit three years of my life - which later turned out to be five. I had no domestic ties. I often thought that the married missionaries had a particularly difficult task trying to balance family life with arduous and dangerous travel.

What did it all achieve?

Sometimes questions are raised whether missionary work has any real benefit. It may appear to upset the lives of a people who are perfectly satisfied until the white man comes along. There is no doubt that northern expansion has brought alcohol, disease, culture clash and environmental problems to a people whom I had found to be very content. Civilization was bound to penetrate the north. Christianity, one can only hope, will lead its people through the inevitable maze of a modern, troubled world. The gospel does not automatically promise a safe haven, a quiet bay in which our lives may shelter, but rather it does guarantee an anchor - a mooring line to which we can cling however violent the storms of life may be.

I have never for a moment regretted my days in the Arctic. I am not, and never have been, a careerist always looking to future prospects and advancements. For me, the important task lies in today. It really never occurred to me that missionary work might impose any sort of penalty - I would have gone anyway! It was very revealing that, sometime later, when I was trying to find a parish, one bishop who interviewed me remarked, "Your time in the north is all very well, but what you now need is the discipline of a good, tough curacy." My wife was with me on that occasion and as she never stood in awe of bishops, her response was immediate: "He has already done two curacies, with city and country experience, and five years in the mission field. How many of your clergy can offer you that?" There was a prolonged silence followed by a genuine apology. Within a few years, when I came to know him better, I developed a high regard for this bishop's gifts and abilities. I like to think that we became close friends.

It is very difficult to assess the contributions, if any, which a priest makes to the spiritual lives of others. It must be very heartening for a doctor to see the achievements which he has made during his lifetime: he has saved many lives, cured many illnesses and can look back upon years of fulfilment. He deals with the body and can see the physical evidence of his role in people's lives. It is much more perplexing to gauge the success of spiritual efforts. Sometimes they are quite evident and that is very rewarding, but often we wonder if any impact has been made at all. I have no way of knowing if my five years among the Inuit made any real impression upon their lives. One can only hope that they did. Many years later, when I was retiring from a school chaplaincy, one of the students wrote to me, saying, "I am not a very religious person, but I admire everything you stand for." If this is true, one would hope that if the Inuit could not always understand my preaching in their language, perhaps a small part of the example I struggled to set might remain with them. I would be well satisfied if I have left a little of that legacy in the Arctic. As someone has remarked, "Christianity is caught, not taught."

For my part, the benefits were enormous and totally unexpected. No other "parish" has ever allowed me to share the lives of my people on such an equal footing. Admittedly, when at home, I lived in a mission house while my flock were in tents or igloos, but when I travelled - and I spent most of the year doing just that - my Inuk guide and I were two men sharing the same dangers, deprivations and discomforts. The Arctic became a great equalizer. In a wealthy parish the priest is so often out of step; he cannot possibly enjoy the privileges of his parishioners - even if he wishes to do so. Conversely, in a poor area he is handicapped in a different way; his living conditions may be more comfortable than those of his people.

I have always felt that the clerical collar, the outward symbol of my calling, imposes a great wall between clergy and laity. Its adoption does not automatically change the individual; but rather it does seem to alter the public's perception of us and sometimes their attitude towards us. We are what we are and my profession is still subject to the same temptations, desires and hopes common to humanity. I am not attempting to downplay ordination nor the special role which the priesthood is called upon to fulfil. The laying on of hands at ordination gives us a unique status and the vows which we take place us in a "high conduct" category, but it does not change the basic, inner nature of man. We are strengthened by the special gift of the Holy Spirit, but the bishop's hand does not make the priest's armour invincible. I am sure that all clergy are conscious at times in their lives of a personal battle between God and mammon. We all struggle to follow the pattern of Christ, but knowing that we may fall short of the mark should not mean that we abandon the task.

The spartan life of the Arctic taught me great lessons in frugal living. It was a stripped-down, bare-bones existence totally foreign to any previous experience. Possessions and ease of living have become so important in our lives today that the more we have the more we want and the more we consider to be essential. When I reached civilization again, I had a heightened awareness of so many simple pleasures. I well remember the sheer joy of a long tub soak in a warm bathroom with hot running water. Life on $1,200 a year certainly prompted careful household management and wise expenditure; religion has always emphasised the benefits of abstinence and self-denial. It is amazing what one can learn to do without and how much more appreciative one can be of small comforts. It was a great training in putting first things first.

The strongest memories which I carry away with me are those of the Inuit character. The Inuit word "Inuk" literally means "the man," and that is how I shall always think of him - a person unique and supreme in his own environment, creative, mechanical and intelligent. They are a very happy people with a great love of family life and children.

It is many years since I left the north, but I can still recall vivid impressions of the simplicity of daily life and the heroic strength of such lovable, cheerful people living under what most of us might call impossible conditions. The challenge of rudimentary living standards, coupled with an unfriendly environment, promoted, rather than defeated, their inner strengths and capabilities. A white man might be overwhelmed by such hostile circumstances. The Inuit coped magnificently. Their stoicism in accepting the inevitable with dignified calm was an example I shall never forget. I went as a teacher, but came away the pupil.

PRINTED AND BOUND
IN BOUCHERVILLE, QUÉBEC, CANADA
BY MARC VEILLEUX IMPRIMEUR INC.
IN AUGUST, 1997